Ferenc Orbán

GUIDE TO JEWISH HUNGARY

Ferenc Orbán

Guide to Jewish Hungary

Budapest, 2004

PUBLISHED WITH GENEROUS SUPPORT FROM THE
MINISTRY OF NATIONAL CULTURAL HERITAGE

Historical overview revised and complemented by TAMÁS RAJ

English translation by MAGDALÉNA SELEANU

Photographs by KÁROLY SZELÉNYI

Layout, cover design
and illustrations editing by MRS GÉZA BORBÉLY

All rights reserved. No part of this publication may be
reproduced or transmitted in any form or by any means,
electronic or mechanical, including photocopy,
recording or any other information storage and retrieval
system, without prior permission in writing by the publisher.

Copyright © Ferenc Orbán,
Tamás Raj, Károly Szelényi, Magdaléna Seleanu
Makkabi Publishing House Ltd., 2004

ISBN 963 7475 88 5

Published by MAKKABI PUBLISHING HOUSE LTD.
1055 Budapest, Szent István krt. 11.
Tel.: (36 1) 354-1560   Fax: (36 1) 354-1561

Distributed by BIBILICAL WORLD GALLERY
1077 Budapest, Wesselényi utca 13.
Tel.: (36 1) 267-8502
www.makkabi.hu and www.judaica.hu

Printed in Hungary by FERA-PRINT BT. Solymár

Preface

Some eight years ago, the Makkabi Publishing House published a bilingual, Hungarian-English guide to Jewish Hungary *(Jewish life in Hungary)* assembled by one of the present authors. This book turned out to be an important milestone in Jewish community life, and it quickly became quite popular among the growing number of Jewish visitors to Hungary following the political changes in the country. Since then, however, there have been many changes: new institutions and organisations were founded, some of the provincial Jewish communities underwent a welcome revival, calling for the revision and updating of the book. This new edition has made use of the experiences gained during the publication of the original volume and of the many suggestions made by readers. One might even say that the present volume is an entirely new book, printed in a slightly different format and supplemented with many colour illustrations. The superb new photographs were made by one of the best known Hungarian photographers, Károly Szelényi (Magyar Képek Publishing House). We have also included a series of archive photos in the book.

In contrast to the previous volume, we published the Hungarian version of the book separately (in summer, 2003); the English version has been extensively revised and expanded compared to the Hungarian edition. The English edition is more detailed because we felt that visitors from abroad should be offered more in the way of historical background and tourist information. We have naturally also taken into consideration new suggestions and corrections. We would greatly appreciate if readers would continue to help our work with their ideas and suggestions, and possible corrections that we could include in future editions.

The first part of the book offers a significantly more detailed overview of Hungarian Jewish history. This is followed by a detailed gazetteer of Hungarian Jewish organisations, Jewish communities, educational, cultural and welfare organisations, as well as of the restaurants and other amenities available to Hungarian and foreign visitors. The third part of the volume is the guide-book proper, with suggested itineraries for visiting the Jewish sights and monuments in Budapest and the provinces. It is our hope that we can also offer less-known, new information about various monuments, sight and other memorial places for visitors of Hungarian origin.

Readers and visitors interested in additional information, such as the Jewish monuments of a particular town, should not hesitate to contact the Jewish community of the area or the Alliance of the Jewish Congregations of Hungary (MAZSIHISZ). Makkabi Publishing House Ltd. has recently launched its website (www.zsido.hu), offering a wide range of information, a chat forum and a discussion board.

In order to facilitate the use of this book, we have used various pictograms to complement the text with additional information. The four maps accompanying the text are intended to help orientation. The numbering on these maps and the pictograms are included beside the description of a particular monument, sight, etc., as well as beside the suggested stops of the recommended itinearies. The explanation of these pictograms and the key to the maps can be found at the end of the book. The Budapest map also includes a few sights that have not been separately mentioned; an explanation is provided at the back.

We hope our readers will enjoy the book and we wish our visitors a memorable visit!

Budapest, February 2004.

Makkabi Publishing House Ltd.

The Szeged synagogue on an old postcard

History of Hungarian Jewry

Roman Age

Jews first settled in Hungary during the second and third centuries CE, when the western part of the country was part of the Roman province of Pannonia. The epigraphic material recovered from Roman camps and towns provide ample evidence for the Jews' settlement here.

A part of the province's Jewish population arrived as merchants from Rome, while others were brought here as slaves, directly from Palestine. Three legions were transferred from Pannonia to Judea in order to quell the uprising led by Bar Kochba (132–135). These troops later brought the slaves drafted into auxiliary units to the garrison in Aquincum (Óbuda, part of modern Budapest) where they were subsequently stationed, and Savaria (modern Szombathely). The presence of Pannonian legions in Palestine is evidenced by a Roman memorial plaque from near Bethar, where Bar Kochba made a final stand, and a coin minted by Bar Kochba, brought to light from the grave of a Roman soldier uncovered near Komárom, now in the Numismatic Collection of the Hungarian National Museum.

It is therefore hardly surprising that there were flourishing Jewish communities in Hungary well before the Hungarian Conquest in 895. The Roman finds from Intercisa (modern Dunaújváros) included a memorial plaque erected sometime around 225 by Cosimus, leader of the customs station, in honour of his mother, Julia; according to the plaque, Cosimus was the "prefect of the Jewish synagogue" and of the local Jewish community (the plaque is currently housed in the Hungarian National Museum).

A gravestone in the Budapest Jewish Museum preserves the memory of a family (father, mother and child). In addition to a portrait of the deceased, depicted in relief, the gravestone also bears a Latin inscription, the depiction of three menorahs and the text "The Lord is One", written in Greek, no doubt expressing their commitment to their faith and to the Jewish community. This gravestone was brought to light at Aquincum.

Oil lamps, gems and other articles decorated with depictions of a menorah have been found in Savaria, lying on the western confines of Hungary, and in other Roman towns (Sopianae/Pécs, Dombóvár, Siklós, Mursa/Eszék), documenting the Jews' presence in these areas during the Roman Age. Finely carved seals owned by Jews have been recovered near the Iseum, a sanctuary dedicated to the goddess Isis in Savaria, where there is still an active synagogue. The graves of a cemetery from the fourth century uncovered at Sárvár in Transdanubia did not yield any gravestones, but the eastward orientation of the deceased and a few other features indicated that the burial ground had been used by a Jewish community.

The Middle Ages

The ancient Hungarian tribes came into contact with the Khazars, who had converted to Judaism, during their sojourn in *Etelköz,* named after Itil, the Khazars' capital on the Volga. When the ancient Hungarians continued their migration towards the Carpathian Basin, two Khazar tribes, the so-called Kabars joined them. Árpád, leader of the Hungarian tribes at the time of the Conquest (895), had taken a Kabar woman as one of his wives. Graves from the Hungarian Conquest period containing articles reflecting the observance of Jewish customs have been uncovered at Békéscsaba.

A letter written by Hasdai ibn Shaprut, a Jewish dignitary in the service of the Caliph of Cordova, suggests that in addition to the Jewish merchants passing through the country, many Jews had already settled in Hungary. There is documentary evidence from the time of the foundation of the medieval Hungarian state indicating the presence of Jews and Jewish communities in Hungary. King St. Stephen, founder of the Hungarian state, who had converted to Christianity and made Christianity the dominant religion, ensured equality between the different peoples and religions in the country (including the Jews).

The number of Jews settling in thriving towns increased, leading to the emergence of the so-called "historical Jewish communities" in Buda, Óbuda, Esztergom, Sopron, and Tata. Unlike their brethren in Western Europe, the Jews of Hungary were not persecuted, most likely because the rulers made good use of the Jews' economic expertise and they also needed their tax for ensuring the kingdom's prosperity and, later, for re-building the country. The Jews were occasionally expelled from a town – usually from the ones inhabited by German settlers – but they were soon allowed to return. In 1093, King Coloman Beuclerc issued laws prohibiting mixed marriages and work on Sundays. Jews were only allowed to settle in episcopal seats – later, they were allowed to buy houses in the free royal towns.

This practice remained in force under the Árpád Dynasty (until 1301). Pressured by the Pope (and the German merchant towns), King Endre forbade mixed marriages, ordered the wearing of a special badge (enacted by the Lateran Council of 1215), and prohibited the Jews from holding certain offices and from receiving titles of nobility in the Golden Bull (1222) and in the Bereg Oath (1233), although he continued to make use of the Jews' economic services. A distinguished Jewish count of the chamber called Teka is known to have been active in western Hungary. King Béla IV, Endre's son and successor on the throne, rescinded these restrictive decrees owing to the Mongolians' imminent attack and the devastation following the Mongolian invasion (1241–42) in order to enlist the Jews' economic help for defending the country.

In 1239, King Béla IV appealed to the Pope that the public revenues be again farmed by the Jews, for "this was the king's and country's interest". Pope Gregory IX reluctantly permitted the relaxation of the restrictions imposed on the the Jews of Hungary after the Hungarian king's repeated appeals. From this time on (under King Béla IV and his son, King Stephen V), a number of coins with Hebrew legend were minted, with the Hebrew letters designating the name of the minter, or the farmer of the mining revenues, or the location of the mint. In addition to coins with Hebrew legends, seals and rings inscribed with Hebrew letters, indicating the Jews' privileged status, are also known from this period. King Béla IV's letter of privilege for the Jews, issued in 1251, was confirmed by subsequent rulers of the medieval Kingdom of Hungary. As "servants of the Royal Chamber" *(servi camerae),* the Jews paid their taxes directly to the king, and they were legally directly under royal jurisdiction The Jews of Hungary were engaged in trade and monetary transactions, and the royal court often relied heavily on their financial resources and expertise.

The earliest tombstone inscribed with Hebrew letters is known from Buda; it was erected by Pesach, son of Peter, in 1278. By this time, there were important Jewish communities in Buda, Sopron, Kőszeg, Esztergom, Székesfehérvár and several other towns. The remains of medieval Jewish synagogues have been uncovered in Sopron and Buda. One of the medieval synagogues in Sopron dates to the thirteenth century, the other to the fourteenth century. A separate women's prayer room *(Frauenschul)* and the rooms of a ritual bath were also identified. These synagogues and the Jewish gravestones found by them can be seen in Új Street in Sopron.

Under the reign of King Louis the Great (from the House of Angevin), the Jews were forced to briefly leave Hungary (1360–64). When the exiles were allowed to return, the king placed them under royal protection, conforming to the practice of his predecessors. Many Jews immigrated to Hungary from Western Europe, where they were persecuted and charged with false accusation, such as blood libels and poisoning wells, in the wake of the bubonic plague sweeping through Europe in 1381. The Jews of Buda first settled around *Szombat* [Shabbat] Gate, a name believed to have originated from the Jews' practice of closing the gate on Saturdays, the Jewish day of rest. From the reign of King Louis the Great, the Jews lived in Táncsics Mihály Street (called Judengasse, or Jewish Street in the Middle Ages).

Although the Jews were again subjected to certain restrictions under King Sigismund of Luxembourg, they were now allowed to settle on nobles' estates in addition to the royal towns. The great synagogue of Buda, rising above the town walls, was built at this

The Szekszárd synagogue on an old postcard

time; this unusual Gothic building could be seen from afar by travellers approaching the town along the Vienna road or on the Danube. (The synagogue is one of the most prominent buildings on contemporary engravings depicting the Buda townscape.)

The golden age of medieval Jewry in Hungary coincided with the prosperity under the reign of King Matthias. From the 1470s until the Battle of Mohács in 1526, a period characterized by cultural influences of the Italian Renaissance in Hungary, the members of the Mendel family, a wealthy, prominent Jewish family of Spanish ancestry from Germany, held the post of the leader of the Buda community and of the Jewish Prefect, an office instituted by King Matthias.

According to the description of an anonymous knight from Erfurt, the Jews participated in the wedding procession held on the occasion King Matthias' marriage to Beatrix of Naples in 1476: at the entrance of the Castle of Buda, "the Jews were led by their aged prefect riding a horse with his drawn sword, from which hung a basket containing ten pounds of silver. Riding beside him was his son, with his sword and a silver basket. Behind them came twenty-four knights, all dressed in purple garments, their caps decorated with three ostrich feathers." According to this description, Mendel Fekete (Schwartz), his son Jacob and the "knights" (no doubt the dignitaries of the community) appeared with a flag bearing the Star of David in the marriage procession. (As a matter of fact, this is one of the rare documented instances of the Star of David used as a symbol of Jewry.) The description of the procession reflects the special status of Hungarian Jews – we know of no other instance in medieval Europe, when the Jews were allowed to appear in public riding a horse and bearing a sword.

Following King Matthias' death in 1490, Hungary was increasingly threatened by the expansion of the Ottoman Empire. The Jews' position became uncertain and there were outbursts of persecution. Even so, a Jew by the name of Imre Szerencsés (Fortunatus) (originally called Shlomo ben Ephraim) became treasurer to King Louis II, the last Hungarian sovereign, who fell during the Battle of Mohács. Although Fortunatus was forced to convert because of his liaison with a Christian woman, he continued to help his Jewish brethren. István Werbőczy's famed law-code, the *Tripartitum,* containing various anti-Jewish measures, was assembled at this time. It is an ironic twist of fate that when he died in October 1541, right after the Turkish siege of Buda, he was buried by the pious Jews of Buda in their own cemetery.

The Ottoman period

After 1526, following the Turkish victory at Mohács, Hungary was divided into three parts and anarchy reigned supreme everywhere. In the westerly regions remaining under royal jurisdiction, the Jews were expelled from Sopron and Kőszeg – they fled to the neighbouring Esterházy and Nádasdy estates, finding refuge in Kismarton, Nagymarton, Sopronkeresztúr (called *Tzelem* in Hebrew), Köpcsény,

Kabold, Boldogasszony and Rohoc. (After settling in these settlements, the exiles litigated with the two towns for some three hundred years, until the latter were obliged to let them return in 1840.) Although the Jews expelled from Kőszeg had every reason to be bitter, they played a crucial role in the successful defence of the town (organised by the Croatian Miklós Jurisich) as military suppliers at the time of the Ottoman attack in 1532.

The Jews of Buda left the town in 1526, returning only in 1541, when it fell to the Turks. Their resettlement was commemorated in a Hebrew inscription on the synagogue's foundation stone: ש'א בת פ ("301 [=1541], in the eightieth year of the synagogue"). This inscription reveals that the great synagogue of Buda had been built in 1461, under King Sigismund.

With the exception of a few major towns, most Hungarian Jews lived in villages under the protection of nobles during the Ottoman period. They were engaged in farming taxes, or leasing inns or landholdings, many were merchants or simple peddlers. The German town burghers (artisans and merchants) regarded them as serious competitors and tried to oust them from the market. Anti-Jewish pogroms are known to have occurred in Upper Hungary (present-day Slovakia), in Nagyszombat, Bazin and elsewhere. The Jews in the Turkish-occupied territories of Hungary lived under far more agreeable circumstances than their brethren in the Kingdom of Hungary. In Transylvania, a principality with fairly wide autonomy subordinate to the Sublime Porte, the Reformation brought an unprecedented religious tolerance and a general friendliness towards the Jews. Simon Péchi, former chancellor of Transylvania, launched a Judaizing "Sabbatarian" movement on his own estates in Bözödújfalu, a village inhabited by Hungarian Széklers, exhorting his Christian people to practice the Biblical Jewish faith. Péchi translated the Psalms and the Jewish prayer-book into Hungarian. (The Transylvanian Sabbatarians converted to Judaism after the emancipation of the Jews, and they had to suffer persecution and deportation during the Holocaust.)

In addition to the Jews who returned to Buda, Sephardic Jews from other Turkish occupied territories (Belgrade, Istanbul, Bulgaria, and Syria) too settled in the town. They established a separate synagogue for themselves in the house of the former Jewish Prefect at 26 Táncsics Street. (This building and the so-called Syrian synagogue used by this community is now a museum. An exhibition of Jewish gravestones from the Ottoman period can be seen in the museum's entrance hall.)

In the mid-seventeenth century, the Jewish community of Buda grew into a major, flourishing cultural centre. Renowned scholars, rabbis and Cabbalists, Hebrew and Yiddish poets lived in the town. Outstanding among them was Ephraim Cohen, head of the Buda *yeshiva*, and his two sons-in-law: Zvi Ashkenazi, the later Sephardic chief rabbi of Amsterdam, and Isaac Schulhof, who in his chronicle of Buda *(Megillat Ofen)*, recorded the life and the later plight of the Jewish community.

Two depictions and inscriptions from the Hebrew Bible were discovered on the arch above the entrance to the Syrian synagogue: a Star of David painted with red (a colour believed to have magical properties), and the Cabbalist version of the Aaron's prayer. The other depiction was a bow, also in red, with the words of Hannah's prayer: "The bows of the mighty men are broken, and they that stumbled are girded with strength" (1Samuel 2: 4). These depictions reflect a sense of some imminent danger and the Cabbalistic beliefs of the community. Two ceremonial swords, one with a silver, the other with a golden hilt, inscribed with a Hebrew text, are also known from this period, indicating both the Jews' desperate readiness to defend themselves and, again, their Cabbalistic convictions. (The silver-hilted sword, found first, was for a long time mistakenly believed to have belonged to the prefect Mendel.)

Following the Turks' unsuccessful Vienna campaign in 1683, the allied Christian army besieged Buda in 1684 and then again in 1686. The latter proved successful: Buda was occupied. The Jewish community was plundered and practically wiped out on September 2–3, 1686. The Jews participated in the defence of the town during both sieges.

In his chronicle, Schulhof describes in detail the dismal situation in which the Jews found themselves between 1683 and 1686: living in the borderland between the two empires, they prospered, but the danger of destruction hovered constantly above their heads. Schulhof described the 1686 siege, in the course of which the greater part of the populous Jewish community (including his own wife and child) were cruelly massacred by the conquerors.

The great synagogue was besieged by the Christian troops, and since they were unable to defeat the Jews, they simply set the building on fire. In 1964, when the synagogue was excavated, a number of charred corpses were found under the ruins. (These corpses were eventually laid to rest in the Jewish cemetery of Rákoskeresztúr.) Following the expulsion of the Turks, a part of the Jewish population living in the formerly Turkish occupied parts of Hungary too left for the Turkish Empire.

After the expulsion of the Turks

Following the recapture of Buda in 1686, Hungary came under Habsburg rule. The Jews were not allowed to settle in the major towns, and through the goodwill of great the landowners they therefore moved to the major estate centres, then to the towns emerging and growing at the intersection of major trade routes. At first, Jews could only enter Pest and Buda on the weekly market day and during fairs – they were allowed to stay at Óbuda owing to the benevolence of the Zichy counts. Hungary's more westerly and easterly regions, greatly depopulated in the wake of the Turkish wars, were settled by German, Slovak and other ethnic groups, as well as Jews, the latter arriving from Bohemia, Moravia, Poland and, later, Galicia, after this region became part of the Austrian Monarchy. The former called themselves *oberländer* and spoke German and Yiddish, while the latter came to be called *unterländer* and spoke Hungarian and an eastern Yiddish dialect.

In 1769, the Jews of Hungary numbered about 20,000, a figure that rose to 80,000 by 1787. The Jews were mostly engaged in the trade of agricultural products, buying and selling wine, grain, leather and other commodities from the large estates and villages.

During the uprising against the Habsburgs led by Prince Ferenc Rákóczi II (1703–1711), the Jews living in western Hungary became the suppliers of the imperial forces, while their brethren in the country's eastern part of the rebellious kuruc troops. Important Jewish communities flourished in northeastern Hungary during the eighteenth century; their members were simple, pious folk (lumberers, raftsmen, wagoners, village shopkeepers and peddlers), most of whom joined the Hassidic movement. Jews had originally settled in the Hegyalja region, renowned for its wine production, to supply their brethren in Poland and Russia with kosher wine. Soon they organised the export and international trade of the entire wine-growing region, contributing to the fame of the wines produced here.

In western Hungary, the Jewish population was characterised both by a strict commitment to Jewish traditions and Jewish learning, and by a cultural openness to modernisation; most of the Jews earned their living as arendars (leasing land, inns, distilleries, mills and the like), merchants, non-guilded craftsmen (glaziers, jewellers, watch-makers, gilders, and the like) or as musicians. Renowned klezmer bands and musicians were active in Hungary, some of whom were immortalised by Mihály Csokonai Vitéz, the best known poet of this period. Márk

Rózsavölgyi (1787–1848), the perhaps most famous Jewish musician, was the composer of the *palotás* dance-tune played at the opening ceremony of the National Theatre. (He was originally the leader of a klezmer band.)

The first representative of Hassidism in Hungary was Isaac Taub, the *tzaddik* of Nagykálló, living in the late eighteenth century. Many legends have survived about him. He lived together with the peasants and herdsmen of the region, whose customs and songs he incorporated into his teachings. The Szatmár folksongs, such as "The rooster is crowing" and "The lambs are crying", are still sung in Hungarian by the rabbi's follower throughout the world. Many renowned *tzaddiks*, such as Moses Teitelbaum of Sátoraljaújhely, Sájele Steiner of Bodrogkeresztúr and Herman Friedländer, were active in the region in later times too; their graves are regularly visited by their followers.

During the War of the Austrian Succession, Maria Theresa (1740–1780) imposed a so-called tolerance tax *(taxa tolerantialis)* on the Hungarian Jews (without the approval of the Hungarian Diet), originally intended to contribute to the war effort. This tax was not abolished after the war ended; the amount of the tax was continuously increased, from 20 thousand gold florins in 1749 to 50 thousand in 1772, reaching 160 thousand by 1813. The Hungarian counties refused to participate in collecting this illegal special tax and thus it proved impossible to collect it after 1828.

Joseph II (1780–1790) decreed that the Jews should take German surnames as part of the imperial policy of Enlightenment, and he also ordered the establishment of German language schools for the Jewish community. The Jewish Enlightenment (Haskalah) thus also spread among Hungarian Jewry. Many joined the circle of Moses Mendelssohn, the German Jewish philosopher, and their followers took their lead. They included the poet Salamon Löwissohn (1788–1821), the proof-reader of the Anton Schmidt printing house in Vienna and author of many educational books, Saphir Moritz Gottlieb (1796–1858), who in his youth wrote a Yiddish Purimspiel while still living in Óbuda and after moving first to Austria and later to Germany, became a celebrated German satirist and critic.

The drive for reform among Hungarian Jewry could also be noted in religious issues: the leader of Reform Jews was Áron Chorin (1766–1844), while the Conservative movement was headed by Moses Münz (1750–1831), rabbi of the magnificent synagogue in Óbuda, and Moses Schreiber-Sofer (1762–1839), the renowned rabbi of Pozsony. Supporters of the Reform movement would have preferred to renew the liturgy, as well as the traditional architecture and layout of the synagogue, for example by moving the *bimah* (the raised platform with the desk from which the Torah is read), from its traditional place in the centre of the synagogue to the eastern wall to resemble an altar. (One fine example of traditional architecture is the Apostag synagogue built in the later eighteenth century.) There were heated debates on the use of organs and choirs in the synagogue and, also, on the introduction of Hungarian as the language of the sermons.

THE AGE OF REFORM, THE 1848–49 WAR OF INDEPENDENCE AND THE EMANCIPATION

In the early nineteenth century, known as the Age of Reform, the liberal nobilty embraced the cause of civic reform, the abolition of the vestiges of Feudalism and, also, the emancipation of the Jews. The issue of the Jews' emancipation was often raised at the Diet, but many decades elapsed before the law was enacted. As a result of their immense contribution to the growth of national industry and trade created by them, the Jews gradually became part of the country's economic life. For example, Izsák Lőwy (1793–1847) founded his tanning factory on a piece of barren land he purchased from the Károlyi counts, from which there eventually evolved a new, modern settlement with an independent council, no religious discrimination and an industry unfettered by the restrictions imposed by traditional craft guilds. Named Újpest [New Pest] by Lőwy, the settlement grew into a sizeable town with an important Jewish community: its first synagogue was built in 1839. (Újpest is currently part of District IV in the northern part of Budapest. Over twenty thousand Jews were deported from here during the Holocaust.)

In 1839, Mór Fischer Farkasházi (1800–1880) founded the world famous Herend porcelain factory, whose magnificent sets later adorned the table of Queen Victoria amongst others. His son, Vilmos Fischer Farkasházi (1839–1921) settled in Kolozsvár, becoming a leading figure of Hungarian industry in Transylvania – at the millennial celebration, commemorating the one thousandth anniversary of the foundation of the Hungarian state, he represented the industrialists of Transylvania. The Deutsch & Son company, established in 1822, built Hungary's first sugar refinery.

Led by Lajos Kossuth, the liberal nobility of the Age of Reform supported the idea of Jewish emancipation: in 1840, the Diet decreed that the Jews could freely settle throughout Hungary (with the exception of the mining towns) and they were allowed to found factories and trade. Móric Bloch (1815–1891), who changed his name to Mór Ballagi and later became a member of the Academy, published a bilingual Hebrew-Hungarian Bible in 1840. The most outstanding rabbis published bilingual prayer-books and religious textbooks, and delivered their sermons in Hungarian. Lipót Löw (1811–1875), who later served as a chaplain during the 1848-49 War of Independence, arrived to Nagykanizsa from Czernahora in Moravia in 1841. Three years later, he preached exclusively in Hungarian. The first Hungarian Jewish yearbook was published in 1848.

The Jewish participation in the 1848–49 War of Independence that broke out on March 15, 1848, exceeded by far the Jews' proportion within the country's population as regards their numbers in the army and their financial contribution to the revolutionary cause. According to Kossuth's declaration in Jászberény, about 20 thousand Jews fought in the 180 thousand strong *honvéd* army: seventy-six served as lieutenants, twenty-nine as first lieutenants, thirty as captains and eight as majors. There were altogether fifty-six Jewish field surgeons, and in addition to Lipót Löw, Arszlán Schwab (1794–1857), Chief Rabbi of Pest and one of the outstanding leaders of the

Reform movement, and Ignác Eichorn (1825–1875) too served as chaplains. (The former were imprisoned after the War of Independence was crushed, while Eichorn followed Kossuth into the emigration. Following the Compromise of 1867, he returned to Hungary, changed his name to Ede Horn and was appointed deputy undersecretary of commerce.) We must also mention Ede Reményi, Artúr Görgey's aid-de-camp, who became a renowned violinist and composer in New York. (Reményi can be credited with creating the fund for the statue of István Széchenyi and Sándor Petőfi, two of the most outstanding Hungarians of the period.) At its last session on July 28, 1849 in Szeged, the National Assembly enacted the emancipation of the Jews. Sadly, this law could not be enforced owing the fall of the War of Independence.

In view of the Jewish community's support of the War of Independence, it is not mere chance that Haynau, the merciless butcher of Brescia, noted that "by their passion and wicked deeds, the Jews supported the Hungarian revolution to such an extent that it could hardly have gained the importance it did without their participation." Following the suppression of the revolution, a huge collective fine was imposed on the Jewish communities. (Following the Compromise of 1867, this sum was reimbursed by Emperor Francis Joseph I in the form of an educational fund. The Budapest Rabbinical Seminary and the Teacher Training College, inaugurated in 1877, were built from this fund.)

Following the Compromise of 1867 and the creation of the Austro-Hungarian Monarchy, the bill on

Jewish emancipation was passed, granting the Jews full political and civic rights. The General Jewish Congress was convened with the aim of creating a uniform Jewish organisation. However, three organisations emerged instead: the largest was that of Congress or Neolog (Reform) Jewry, followed by Conservative (Orthodox) Jewry and the communities which did not join either side, known as Status Quo Jewry (whose name and slogan was *status quo ante,* expressing their position that the situation should remain unchanged: they opposed both the introduction of reforms and of additional religious restrictions.) The full recognition and reception of the Jewish religion was only achieved later, in 1895.

The great Neolog synagogue in Dohány Street was built earlier, in 1859; Ferenc Liszt played on its organ. The main synagogue of the Status Quo community stood nearby, in Rumbach Sebestyén Street. Built in 1872, it remains the single Hungarian building designed by Otto Wagner, the pioneer of the Viennese Art Nouveau. The great Orthodox synagogue and the office building of the Orthodox community in Kazinczy Street, designed by the Löffler brothers, were built in 1913. While the centre of the Neolog and the Orthodox movement was in Budapest, the Status Quo community chose Debrecen as its seat. The most admired rabbi of the Dohány Street Synagogue was Simon Hevesi (1868–1943), that of the Rumbach Street synagogue was Illés Ádler (1868–1924) and that of the Kazinczy Street synagogue was Koppel Reich (1838–1930). (Together with Immanuel Löw of Szeged, Koppel Reich became a member of the Upper House of

Hungarian Parliament in 1927; owing to his age, he should have been the chairman by seniority, but the political atmosphere of the period made this impossible.) The best-known cantors of the Dohány Street synagogue were Quartin and Manó Ábrahámssohn; that of the Rumbach Street synagogue was Israel Tkatsch from Tarnopol. The first widely known cantor was Jossele Rosenblatt, who had emigrated to the United States from Pozsony around the turn of the century.

Development until the end of World War 1

Budapest emerged from the unification of three towns (Buda, Pest and Óbuda) in 1873. The Jews' contribution to the city's rise and prosperity was considerable. Hungary's economy was undergoing a period of growth, in which the Hungarian Jews played an important role. They built many factories (including the Wolfner tanning factory, the Pick and Herz salami factories), they opened mines, founded banks, participated in the creation of a railway network and organised the modern export of Hungarian agricultural produce, fruits and wine. (Suffice it here to mention Wodianer's model farm in Maglód and the wholesale fruit trade organised by Hercz Kecskeméti in the Kecskemét area.)

Hungarian Jewry also played a major role in the development of Hungarian sciences, especially the medical sciences. The first Jewish doctor graduating from Budapest University, József Östereicher Manes was the first balneologist active in the Lake Balaton region, who founded the settlement and the Hospital of Cardiology at Balatonfüred. The pioneer of Hungarian ophthalmology, Ignác Hirschler (1823–1891), one of the main organisers and chairman of the General Jewish Congress of 1868–69, was elected member of the Hungarian Academy of Sciences and also became a member of the Upper House. The same rank was achieved by the leading figure of modern Hungarian pulmanology, Baron Frigyes Korányi (1823–1913) who served as a field surgeon during the 1848–49 War of Independence. The outstanding figure of modern Hungarian surgery, Baron Manó Herczel (1861–1918), was active as the chief surgeon of the Szent István Hospital. The pioneers of Hungarian linguistics include Bernát Munkácsi (1860–1937); Ignác Goldziher achieved lasting fame as one of the founders of modern Islamic scholarship, while Ignác Acsády (1845–1906) and Henrik Marcali (1856–1943) both gained distinction as historians.

In 1895, Hungarian Parliament proclaimed Judaism an acknowledged denomination *(recepta religio),* on par with the other ones. Another law on civil marriage, enabling Jewish-Christian mixed marriages, was passed the same year. Increasingly more Jews defined themselves as Hungarians, most of whom were registered as Hungarians of the Mosaic faith during the censuses taken in the multi-ethnic parts of the country. In these regions, the Jews usually voted for the Hungarian deputies. The general process of Magyarisation was not halted even by the Tiszaeszlár blood libel and the activity of Győző Istóczy's Anti-Semitic Party.

At the close of the nineteenth century, Hungary underwent an unprecedented growth, and by the early twentieth century the country even eclipsed her Western European neighbours in certain fields. There can be no doubt that Hungarian Jewry played a major role in this prosperity. Some 280 Jewish families were ennobled, twenty-six of whom were granted the title of baron. Nowhere else in Europe did Jews enter the ranks of the nobility in such great numbers – although it must be borne in mind that nowhere else did they strive to attain nobility.

Hungarian Jewry played an important part in the renewal of Hungarian culture. The most significant literary journal at the turn of the century, *A Hét* [The Week], was launched and edited by the poet József Kiss (1843–1921), while Adolf Ágai (1836–1916) began the publication of *Borsszem Jankó,* a weekly that soon became the best-known satirical paper. The editor-in-chief of *Pesther Lloyd,* Miksa Falk (1828–1908) was elected to the Hungarian Academy of Sciences; he also published the political writings of István Széchenyi (called the "greatest Hungarian" by his contemporaries), he acted as secretary to the "nation's sage", Ferenc Deák and was Empress Elisabeth's Hungarian tutor. The popular *Tolnai Világlapja* [Tolnai's World Journal] and *Tolnai Világlexikon* [Tolnai's World Encyclopaedia] were both edited by the journalist Simon Tolnai (1868–1944), who perished at Mauthausen.

Jews were active in all genres of modern art (in architecture, in sculpture and in painting). Lipót Baumhorn (1860–1932), a student of Ödön Lechner, designed a total of twenty-four magnificent synagogues in the Art Nouveau style, including the splendid synagogue in Szeged (1903). Modern art even made its way into Jewish cemeteries, known for their conservatism: Béla Lajta (1873–1920) designed the gate of the cemetery on Salgótarjáni Road. The crypt of Sándor Schmidl in the Rákoskeresztúr cemetery is one of the outstanding creations of Hungarian Art Nouveau. The new, creative literary wave (led by the poet Endre Ady) first flowed from the pages of the periodical *Nyugat* [West], founded in 1908 by Miksa Fenyő (1877–1972), Ignotus (b. Hugo Veigelsberg, 1869–1949) and Baron Lajos Hatvany (1880–1961).

The peaceful development until the close of World War 1 stimulated the assimilation and strengthening of Hungarian Jewry. There emerged a fairly large well schooled, educated layer of intellectuals, entrepreneurs and merchants, which regarded the country as its homeland, and had no problem in reconciling their Hungarianness with their Jewishness. Hungarian Jewry made a lasting contribution to the creation and growth of Hungarian industry and trade. The list of financiers, economists, scientific researchers, engineers and inventors is impressive by any standard. Jewish writers, poets, artists, actors, directors, film and theatre professionals have forever written their name into the annals of Hungarian culture. Similarly to other European countries, Hungarian Jewry too could at last reveal its immense creative powers, which had been artificially suppressed for many centuries. Unlike the Jews living a traditional lifestyle in rural villages, they actively contributed to the emergence of an urban culture, and a specifically Hungarian-Jewish culture in Budapest.

Many Jews played an active role in politics. Mór Wahrmann (1832–1892), grandson of Izrael Wahrmann, the first rabbi of Pest, rose to become president of the Budapest Chamber of Commerce and Industry and he also acted as president of the Jewish community. Vilmos Vázsonyi (1868–1926) was the first Jew in Hungary to become Minister of Justice, while Baron Samu Hazai (1851–1942), a general of the Hungarian army, was appointed Minister of Defence. Baron József Szterényi (1861–1941), son of Albert Stern, rabbi of Újpest, one of the re-organisers of Hungarian industry, became a secretary of state and, later, Minister of Trade. (Szterény was arrested and imprisoned during the Hungarian Soviet Republic in 1919; later, in 1927, he became a representative in the Upper House.)

Jews were highly represented among the so-called bourgeois radicals. The leading figure of modern political science, Oszkár Jászi (1875–1957), was a minister without portfolio responsible for the national minorities in Mihály Károlyi's government. Many Jews became involved with the Socialist movement; quite a few leaders of the Hungarian Soviet Republic, formed in March, 1919, were Jews. The counter-revolutionary "whites", opposing the Hungarian Soviet Republic and scheming for its downfall too included a number of Jews. (Fifteen of the seventy-two officers who supported the so-called Counter-Revolutionary Government formed in Szeged were Jews.)

Theodor Herzl (1860–1904) and his friend Max Nordau (b. Miksa Südfeld, 1849–1923), the founders of the Zionist movement unfolding at the turn of the century, were both born in Budapest. Herzl grew up in a house next to the Dohány Street synagogue (on the spot where the Jewish Museum now stands), while Nordau lived in a house on the corner of Wesselényi and Rumbach Streets. The Hungarian Zionists founded their own organisation and journal (*Zsidó Szemle* [Jewish Review]), they had their own youth and sports associations. The best known Jewish sports association in Hungary was the Makkabi Fencing and Athletic Club.

Herzl's cousin, Jenő Heltai (1871–1957), poet and writer, who composed the lyrics for the musicalised version of Sándor Petőfi's epic, *János the Hero,* also did much to popularise movies in Hungary. The first Hungarian Olympic champion, Alfréd Hajós (1878–1955) worked as an engineer. Hungarian Jews were prominently represented among Olympic champions and sports in general; suffice it here to mention the fencer Attila Petschauer (1904–1943), who was conscripted into the forced labour service and perished in the Ukraine. (István Szabó's film, "Sunshine", is in part based on his life.)

Anti-Jewish legislation and the Holocaust

Following World War 1 and the shock over the Treaty of Trianon (June 4, 1920), which stripped the country of about two-thirds of her former territory and of about three million ethnic Hungarians, anti-Semitism flared up in Hungary. The counter-revolution turned against the Jews. Organised bands robbed and murdered Jews throughout the country; in Budapest, for example, Jewish merchants were tortured in the basement of the Britannia Hotel. (The most serious incident, claiming several lives, occurred in Pest county, in an area between Izsák and Orgovány.) Immánuel Löw (1854–1944), the greatly respected, erudite Chief Rabbi of Szeged, who later became a member of the Upper House, was charged with lèse majesté. In 1920, the first anti-Jewish law, the *numerus clausus* bill was passed, restricting the proportion of Jews in the higher institutions of learning to five per cent.

The situation of the Jews did not improve under the consolidation programme introduced by Count István Bethlen. In contrast to the Age of Reform, the ideals of nation and progress were no longer intertwined in the vision of the "Christian" Hungary promoted by Regent Miklós Horthy. The German orientation, the irredentist policy and the effect of the Great Depression of 1929–30 steered Hungary towards Fascism. In vain did the Jews of Budapest build the Heroes' Temple in memory of the Jewish soldiers who fell in the Great War (a synagogue still active today) and in vain did they document their large-scale participation in the Hungarian army with the *Hadviseltek Aranyalbuma* [Golden Album of Jewish Servicemen], political power turned against them. The alliance with Hitler's Germany and Mussolini's Italy, and the country's irredentist policies paved the way for World War 2.

While the country's economic situation improved by the late 1930s, the Jews' situation deteriorated with each anti-Jewish law. (Four such laws were enacted by Hungarian Parliament from 1938, each of which was harsher than the previous one.) Hungary entered the war in the summer of 1941, by declaring war on the Soviet Union, by attacking Yugoslavia and occupying a part of Yugoslavia, after bowing to German pressure (in spite of the earlier Hungarian-Yugoslav Non-Aggression Pact). Excluded from regular army service, Jewish men of military age were drafted into so-called forced labour battalions and were forced to wear a special armband. Often acting upon higher orders, the guards assigned to these labour battalions systematically tortured and murdered the unfortunate Jews; many were driven onto the Russian mine-fields that the mines should explode under their feet and kill them. The "punishment" of these unfortunates included hanging, beating and forcing them to go naked in the harsh winter.

In 1941, a total of ten thousand people were murdered during the so-called Újvidék pogrom (Novi Sad in Yugoslavia). In 1942, about twenty thousand so-called "alien" Jews (Jews who had settled in Hungary after 1913) were deported and brutally murdered in Kamenets-Podolsk in the Ukraine. In consequence of the anti-Jewish laws, most Hungarian Jews were fired from their jobs, stripped of their livelihood, and their very lives were in danger. This was but a foretaste of the terrible catastrophe awaiting Hungarian Jewry. On March 19, 1944, the German army occupied Hungary – and with it came Eichmann and his infamous Sonderkommando to implement the "final solution" to the Jewish question.

The Jews were registered and ordered to wear the yellow badge. The deportation of provincial Jewry was begun, first from Sub-Carpathia (in present-day Ukraine) and then from other parts of the country. In Budapest, the Jews were first herded into houses marked with a yellow star and from there into the ghetto. Following the Romanian capitulation in late August, 1944, the front arrived to Hungary and Minister of Defence Vilmos Nagybaczoni Nagy suspended the deportations. Regent Miklós Horthy tried to extricate the country from the war: in his proclamation issued on October 15, 1944, Horthy announced that Hungary would lay down the arms. The extreme nationalists, the Arrow-Cross Party led by Ferenc Szálasi seized power the very same day with military help from the Germans.

While the advancing Russians troops occupied increasingly larger parts of Hungary, terror was rampant in Budapest. Since trains with deportees could no longer be dispatched, Jews in hiding denounced by their neighbours, and the Jewish men and women rounded up on the streets were driven on foot towards Austria. Very few returned from these "death marches". Surviving members of the forced labour battalions were similarly marched to the west. Many perished on the way or were murdered, including the poet Miklós Radnóti (1909–1945), killed during the march from the Bor death camp, and the literary scholar Antal Szerb (1901–1945).

The inhabitants of the Pest ghetto, numbering some seventy thousand souls, could not be deported (owing to the lack of time); seven thousand died from famine and various diseases. (They were buried in the garden of the Dohány Street synagogue; their memory is preserved by Imre Varga's tree, whose leaves are inscribed with the names of the deceased.) Bands of Arrow-Cross men roamed the city's streets, brutally murdering the Jews and any Hungarians who sheltered them or were suspected of being a member of the resistance. Torture chambers were set up in the basements of the so-called Arrow-Cross houses (such as the Thököly restaurant in Zugló). Many Jews were shot into the icy Danube. (A memorial plaque marks the gate of the one-time ghetto, while the memory of the unfortunate Jews shot into the Danube is preserved by a plaque on the Pest side of Margaret Bride and the Vizafogó.)

In addition to many Hungarian intellectuals (including the highly popular actor Pál Jávor, the singer Katalin Karády and countless others), the embassies of neutral countries too participated actively in saving Jewish lives. Most successful among them was Raoul Wallenberg, secretary of the Swedish embassy (he was later arrested by the Russians and deported to the Gulag). The Swiss diplomat Carl Lutz must also be mentioned, as must the Italian Giorgio Perlasca, who posed as the Spanish consul. (Their humanitarian activity has been honoured by memorials.)

The Pest ghetto was liberated on January 17, 1945; the Buda side was only occupied by the Soviet troops on February 13 (the Germans had blown up the bridges linking the two parts), and the entire country was liberated from the Fascists on April 4, 1945. Over six hundred thousand of the country's almost one million Jews perished during the Holocaust; four hundred thousand of the six hundred thousand Jews who had lived on the territory of present-day Hungary were killed.

THE COMMUNIST DICTATORSHIP AND THE POLITICAL CHANGES

A rather controversial situation followed the liberation from the Nazi rule: a part of the Jews who had returned from the death camps and from the forced labour battalions or who had survived the ghetto joined the Zionist movement, while another part simply wanted to renounce their origins and forget their religion. The surviving members of the Jewish middle class actively participated in rebuilding the country. In 1948, the Communists seized power and they imprisoned or deported the so-called "bourgeois elements" from the cities and sent them into internal exile. The Communists soon staged a series of show-case trials against their own party members too. The Jewish members of the Communist leadership (including the party leader Mátyás Rákosi) tried to play down their origins and were often even harsher towards the Jews than towards others. (The Jewish defendants of the Rajk trial, the perhaps best known show-case trial, were arrested two weeks before the others, which can hardly be regarded a mere coincidence.) Taking his cue from the so-called doctors' trial in Russia, Rákosi too made preparations for staging a Zionist trial, whose main defendant was supposed to have been Zoltán Vas, one of his best friends, with whom he was imprisoned earlier and who served as Commissioner of Public Supply after the war. The trial was shelved after Stalin died in the spring of 1953.

Observant Jews, who remained loyal to their traditions and beliefs, mostly belonged to the poorer layers and they could often barely make ends meet. Their shops were confiscated, their licences were revoked, and their international contacts were forcibly severed. From 1949, pressure from the atheist state grew stronger and practically all religious life was stifled. Jewish leaders and youngsters were constantly harassed by the authorities for so-called "Zionist activities". Religion was restricted to religious ceremonies and the commemoration of the victims of the Holocaust; providing a Jewish education for children was practically impossible.

Many Jews participated in the preparation of the 1956 uprising and the armed resistance following the Soviet invasion. István Angyal, a survivor of Auschwitz, was the leader of the freedom fighter group active in the Tűzoltó Street area. He was later sentenced to death and executed. A few anti-Semitic incidents also occurred during the chaotic days of the uprising. Owing to this and to the bitter experiences gained during the 1950s, many Jews left Hungary.

During the Kádár period, the leaders of the Jewish community were closely controlled by the Office for Religious Affairs, with the result that their efforts were mainly directed at maintaining the central organisations of the community. Observant Jews, adhering to their traditions, were often charged with "religiosity" or, even worse, Zionism. (The last arrest and interrogation of so-called Zionists occurred in the summer of 1986.)

The liberal and democratic part of Hungarian Jewry played a prominent role in the political changes. The first "alternative" Jewish organisation of Central Europe, the Hungarian Jewish Cultural Association (MAZSIKE), was founded in Budapest, in 1988. The Speaker of the first freely elected Hungarian Parliament was György Szabad, the renowned history professor, while the ranks of the MPs included some two dozen Jews. Jews partook in almost all wakes of economic and cultural life. Sadly enough, anti-Semitism, artificially suppressed during the Communist dictatorship, again reared its ugly head.

As a result of the political changes and the upsurge of religious and community life, we may rightly speak of the renaissance of the 80–100 thousand strong Hungarian Jewish community. Zionist organisations, civilian and youth associations, culture, education and sports have mushroomed; a Jewish educational and community network has been formed and the community's international contacts too have strengthened. For the first time in forty-five years, the emphasis is on reclaiming and renovating the community's buildings, rather than on their sale.

During the Six Day War of 1967, Hungary severed all diplomatic ties with Israel under Soviet pressure; in 1989, diplomatic ties were re-established on the ambassadorial level and since then, relations between the two countries have greatly expanded.

The political changes have at last again enabled Hungary's Jewish community to live freely as Jews.

The cohesion of the Jewish community is to some extent also fuelled by a smouldering anti-Semitism. Jewish communities have also been formed in provincial towns, where there were no openly Jewish families. Many youngsters born into mixed marriages have begun the search for their Jewish roots. There are currently four Jewish kindergartens, four schools and one university in Budapest.

The controversies and tensions accompanying the social and political changes are also felt by the Jewish community. There has emerged a self-assertive Jewish layer, loyal to its faith and tradition, proud of the State of Israel and, at the same time, strongly devoted to its homeland, similar to the Western European Jewish communities. The main basis of the survival of Hungary's Jewish community is the return of the younger generations to their Jewish roots.

Gusztáv Zoltai
Executive Director
of the Alliance of Jewish
Congregations
of Hungary and of the Budapest
Jewish Community

András Heisler
President of the Alliance
of Jewish Congregations
of Hungary

Sándor Streit
President of the Jewish
Community of Budapest

Gazetteer of Jewish institutions in Hungary

In addition to their exact designation, the numbers and the pictograms aid the location of various institutions, monuments and sights on the map. The first pictograms indicate whether there is an active congregation (together with possible, associated institutions), followed by the pictograms indicating buildings used for purposes other than their original one.

THE INSTITUTIONS OF THE JEWISH COMMUNITY OF HUNGARY

The observant Jews of Hungary are members of the Neolog or Orthodox Congregation. The elected bodies of the Alliance of the Jewish Congregations of Hungary (MAZSIHISZ) include members of both congregations, while their leadership, rabbinate and administration are separate.

National Jewish organisations

1.

Alliance of the Jewish Congregations of Hungary (MAZSIHISZ)

Address: 1075 Budapest, 12 Síp Street
Tel.: +36 1 342 1335
Fax: +36 1 342 1790
E-mail: csillag13@yahoo.com
Homepage: www.zsidohitkozseg.hu
President: Dr. András Heisler
Executive director: Gusztáv Zoltai

2.

Autonomous Orthodox Community of Hungary

Address: 1072 Budapest, 35 Dob Street
Tel.: +36 1 351 0525, +36 1 351 0524
Fax: +36 1 322 7200
Rabbi: Áron Hoffmann
President: Herman Fixler
Chief Secretary: László Herczog

Established in 1870, the Budapest Orthodox Community had some fifty thousand members before World War 2. Although it joined the uniform community (under Neolog leadership) in 1953 under pressure from the state, it retained its internal independence. In 1995, the community regained its independence.

Budapest Jewish Community (BZSH)
Address: 1075 Budapest, 12 Síp Street
Tel.: +36 1 342 1335
Fax: +36 1 342 1790
President: Sándor Streit
Executive director: Gusztáv Zoltai
Leader of the Rabbinate: Chief Rabbi Róbert Deutsch
Tel.: +36 1 342 1180

SYNAGOGUES AND SYNAGOGUE DISTRICTS IN BUDAPEST

16.

1024 Budapest, 49 Frankel Leó Road (Buda district)
Tel.: +36 1 326 1445
Rabbi: Tamás Verő
President: Péter Tordai

17.

1042 Budapest, 8 Berzeviczy Street (Újpest)
Tel.: +36 1 369 0829
Rabbi: Chief Rabbi László Deutsch
President: Zoltán Rappaport

18.

1061 Budapest, 5 Vasvári Pál Street
(Shas Chevra Congregation, Chabad Lubavits)
Tel.: +36 1 342 1328
Rabbi: Baruch Oberländer
President: Gábor Karádi

19.

1067 Budapest, 3 Hunyadi Square
Tel.: +36 1 342 5322
Rabbi: Chief Rabbi Dr. István Domán
President: Miklós László

20.

1066 Budapest, 23 Dessewffy Street (Orthodox)
Tel.: +36 1 342 2353
Director: László Herczog

21., 22.

1074 Budapest, 2 Dohány Street
District office: 1075 Budapest, 12 Síp Street
Tel.: +36 1 342 2353
Rabbi: Chief Rabbi Róber Fröhlich
President: László Heisler

23.

1072 Budapest, 27 Kazinczy Street (Orthodox)
(entrance from 35 Dob Street)
Tel.: +36 1 351 0525
Rabbi: Áron Hoffman
President: Hermann Fixler

24.

1078 Budapest, 17 István Road (Bethlen Square)
Tel.: +36 1 342 6170
Rabbi: Róbert Deutsch
President: Tamás Kálmán

25.

1084 Budapest, 4 Nagyfuvaros Street
(Józsefváros)
Tel.: +36 1 334 2731
Homepage: www.nagyfuvaros.hu
Rabbi: Zoltán Radnóti
President: Sándor Streit
Community journal: Ígéret

26. Orth

1086 Budapest, 22 Teleki Square (Sephardic)
President: Jakab Glaser

27.

1094 Budapest, 29 Páva Street
(entrance from 27 Bokréta Street)
Tel.: +36 1 215 8796
President: Sándor Szedő Neuwirth

28.

1114 Budapest, 5 Károli Gáspár Square
(Lágymányos)
Tel.: +36 1 361 1965
Leader: Gábor Halmos

29.

1136 Budapest, 3 Hegedűs Gyula Street
(Újlipótváros)
Tel.: +36 1 340 5085
Rabbi: Chief Rabbi Tamás Lőwy
President: Gusztáv Zoltai

30.

1134 Budapest, 55 Dózsa György Road
Tel.: +36 20 366 8737
Rabbi: Sándor Polnauer
President: György Szalai

31.

1132 Budapest, 3 Visegrádi Street
(Pest Shul, Orthodox)
E-mail: info@pestisul.hu
Homepage: www.pestisul.hu
President: Dr. Sándor Varró

32.

1146 Budapest, 83 Thököly Road
(Bet Aharon; Zugló)
Tel.: +36 1 251 3970
Rabbi: Chief Rabbi Péter Kardos
President: Ferenc Orbán

33.

1145 Budapest, 53 Amerikai Road
(synagogue of the nursing home)
Tel.: +36 1 251 5518
President: József T. Szirmai

34.

1185 Budapest, 27 Honvéd Street
(Kispest–Lőrinc)
Tel.: +36 1 291 4669, +36 30 297 1096
President: Gábor Kalota

1203 Budapest, 9 Téglagyár Square
(7 Zamárdi Street; Pesterzsébet–Soroksár–Csepel)
President: György Tamás Kövesi
Executive director: Dániel Jordán
Tel.: +36 1 284 6431, +36 70 209 1007
E-mail: jjnedda@ax.hu

JEWISH COMMUNITIES, CONGREGATIONS AND SYNAGOGUES IN THE PROVINCE

Central Hungarian Regional Group of the Alliance of the Jewish Congregations of Hungary
2750 Nagykőrös, 21 Rákóczi Road
Tel.: +36 53 355 716
E-mail: feldmajerelnok@kozep-zsido.hu
President: Dr. Péter Feldmajer

Baja 6500, 24 Petőfi Street
Tel.: +36 79 323 960
President: Sándor Bloch

Balassagyarmat 2600, 50 Klapka Street
Tel.: +36 35 312 369
Information: Mrs József Bauer

Békéscsaba 2660, 32 Dr. Becsey Oszkár Street
Tel.: +36 66 327 273
President: Dr. Sándor Moskovits

Debrecen 4025, 26 Bajcsy-Zsilinszky Road
Tel.: +36 52 533 273, + 36 52 533 273
President: Dr. Péter Weisz
Executive director: Sándor Halmos

Gyöngyös 3200, 1 Széna Street
Tel.: +36 37 311 812
President: Ferenc Waldner

Győr 9021, 5 Kossuth Lajos Street
Tel.: +36 96 329 032
President: Tibor Villányi

Hódmezővásárhely 6800, 3 Szeremlei Street
Tel.: +36 62 245 702
President: János Vanderstein

Kaposvár 7400, 14 Berzsenyi Street
Tel.: +36 93 420 288
President: Tibor Lipkovics

Karcag 5300, 7 Kertész Street
Tel.: +36 59 400 379, +36 30 9259 594
President: Andor Molnár
Executive director: Oszkár Rosinger

Kecskemét 6000, 2 Kaszap Street
Tel.: +36 76 484 541
Prayer-house: 5 Nagykőrösi Road
President: Dr. Andor Grósz

Keszthely 8360, 14 Bem József Street
Tel.: +36 83 317 206
President: István Goldschmied

Kiskunhalas 6400, 24 Semmelweis Square
Tel.: +36 77 423 489, +36 30 347 3333
President: András Raáb

Makó 6900, 11 Toldi Street
Tel.: +36 62 413 843, +36 62 412 805
President: Mrs Simon Dr. Zsuzsa Baron

Miskolc 3509, 7 Kazinczy Street
Tel.: +36 46 344 884
President: Jenő Freund

Mosonmagyaróvár 9200, 8 Szabadság Road
Tel.: +36 46 344 884
President: László Ligeti

Nagykanizsa 8800, 6 Fő Street
Tel.: +36 93 312 484
President: Dr. István Székely

Nagykőrös 2750, 21 Rákóczi Road
Tel.: +36 53 355 716
President: Sándor Feldmájer

Nyíregyháza 4400, 6 Mártírok Square
Tel.: +36 42 417 939
President: Gábor Kertész

Pápa 8500, 10 Vásár Street
Tel.: +36 89 323 050
President: Kiss László

Pécs 7621, 1 Fürdő Street
Tel.: +36 72 315 881, +36 72 214 863
Rabbi: Chief Rabbi András Schőnberger
President: István Krausz

Salgótarján 3100, 1 Báthori Street
Tel.: +36 32 430 039
Prayer-house: Füleki Road cemetery
President: Dr. László Gótai

Szeged 6722, 20 Gutenberg Street
Tel.: +36 62 423 849
Rabbi: Chief Rabbi Zsolt Markovics
President: Dr. Imre Gráf
Executive director: Dr. András Lednitzky

Szekszárd 7100, 48 Tarsay Housing Estate
Tel.: +36 74 313 164
Elnök: Rezső Mayer

Székesfehérvár 8000, 19 Várkörút
Tel.: +36 22 311 289, +36 20 9553 580
President: Mátyás Jávor

Szolnok 5000, 33 Mária Street
Tel.: +36 56 333 886
President: Dávid Berman
Information: György Klein
Tel.: +36 56 370 819, +36 56 374 466

Szombathely 9700, 9 Batthyányi Square
Tel.: +36 94 312 500
President: Péter Mezei
Community journal: *Szombati Napló*

Vác 2600, 5 Eötvös Street
Tel.: +36 27 318 786
President: János Turai

Veszprém 8200, 7/c Stromfeld Street
Tel.: +36 88 265 232
Executive director: Dr. Zsuzsa Wittmann

Zalaegerszeg, 1 Rákóczi Street
Tel.: +36 92 317 141
President: Vilmos Siklósi

Central organisations

Jewish Social Welfare Foundation of Hungary
1075 Budapest, 12 Síp Street
Tel.: +36 1 269 6695
Fax: +36 1 352 7094

Jewish Heritage of Hungary Public Endowment (MAZSÖK)
1054 Budapest, 3 Tüköry Street
Tel.: +36 1 269 1068
Fax: +36 1 269 1518
E-mail: mazsok@hu.inter.net

Office of Hungary's Chief Rabbi
1085 Budapest, 27 József Boulevard
Tel.: +36 1 267 6388
Fax: +36 1 267 5995
Dr. József Schweitzer, retired Chief Rabbi

Chaplain of the Hungarian Army
1126 Budapest, 21–23 Hűvösvölgyi Street
Tel.: +36 1 200 2335
Head chaplain: Chief Rabbi Róbert Fröhlich, Brigadier General

5.

Federation to Maintain Jewish Culture in Hungary (MAZSIKE)
Office: 1065 Budapest, 16 Révay Street
Tel.: +36 1 311 6666
Fax: +36 1 311 6666
Homepage: www.mazsike.hu
President: Dr. Péter Feldmajer

Founded in 1988, as the first alternative Jewish organisation, its main objective is to promote integration instead of assimilation, as well as the preservation and popularisation of the Jewish cultural heritage.

Zionist Federation of Hungary
1065 Budapest, 16 Révai Street
Tel.: +36 1 311 5412
E-mail: info@cionista.hu
Homepage: www.cionista.hu
President: Dr. Tibor Engländer

Banned in 1948, the Zionist organisation resumed its activity from 1989. The organisation has several member organisations.

Hungarian Union of Jewish Students
1075 Bp., 5. Pf. 353.
Club: 54 Mária Street, IIIrd floor
Tel.: +36 1 411 0572

Fax: +36 1 411 0573
E-mail: info@ujs.hu
Homepage: www.ujs.hu
President: Tamás Jung

WIZO Hungary
1145 Budapest, 39 Kolumbusz Street
Tel.: +36 30 999 8098
President: Erzsébet Simon

Sim Shalom Progressive Jewish Society
1027 Budapest, 5 Csalogány Street
Tel.: +36 1 214 3940
Tel./Fax: +36 1 201 7648
E-mail: salom@vnet.hu
Homepage: www.szimsalom.hu
Rabbi: Katalin Kelemen
President: Dr. Péter Nógrádi
Secretary: Éva Piszker

This congregation represents the Reform movement in Hungary.

6.

Jewish Theological Seminary –
University of Jewish Studies
1084 Budapest, 2 Bérkocsis Street
Tel.: +36 1 318 7049, +36 1 317 2396, +36 1 318 8834
Homepage: www.or-zse.hu
Rector: Chief Rabbi Dr. Alfréd Schöner
Library
Director: Dr. Ferenc Borsányi Schmidt
Tel.: +36 1 267 5415

7.

Scheiber Sándor Elemantary and High School
1145 Budapest, 38–40 Laky Adolf Street
Tel.: +36 1 221 4219, +36 1 221 4219, +36 1 221 4220,
+36 1 221 4227
Tel./Fax: +36 1 221 4215
E-mail: scheiber@scheiber.sulinet.hu
Homepage: www.scheiber.sulinet.hu
Director: Mrs Gábor Réz
Rabbi: Tamás Verő

8.

Lauder Javne Jewish Community School,
Gymnasium, Vocational School, Music School
and Kindergarten
1121 Budapest, 48 Budakeszi Road
Kindergarten: 1121 Budapest, 46 Budakeszi Road
Tel.: +36 1 275 2240, +36 1 275 2241, +36 1 275 2242
Fax: +36 1 275 2610

E-mail: javne@lauder.hu
Homepage: www.lauder.hu
Director: Dr. Anna Szeszler
Judaic studies: Chief Rabbi Tamás Raj

9.

American Endowment School (Kindergarten, Primary School, Gymnasium and Vocational School)
1077 Budapest, 44 Wesselényi Street
Tel.: +36 1 322 2843, +36 1 342 7143, +36 1 322 2427
E-mail: aai@aai-bp.sulinet.hu
Homepage: www. aai-bp.sulinet.hu
Director: Mrs Dr. Artúr Róna
Religious director: Baruch Kaisler

Maintained by the Hungarian Autonomous Orthodox Community, the school offers a traditional Jewish education.

10.

Benjámin Kindergarten of the Budapest Jewish Community
1141 Budapest, 12 Ungvár Street
Tel.: +36 1 251 0577
Director: Mrs Rádai Éva Somosi

College of the Budapest Jewish Community
1065 Budapest, 16 Révay Street
Tel.: +36 1 311 9214
Director: Imre Kárpáti

Chabad Lubavits Jewish Education Association
1075 Budapest, 4 Wesselényi Street
Tel.: +36 1 268 0183
E-mail: info@zsido.com, oberlander@zsido.com
Homepage: www.zsido.com
Director: Rabbi Baruch Oberlander

Gan Menachem Kindergarten and Beis Menachem School
1124 Budapest, 41 Tamási Áron Street
Tel.: +36 1 395 4470
E-mail: ovoda@zsido.com

The association's primary goal is to provide a Jewish education and to promote an awareness of Jewish traditions for both children and adults.

Lauder International Jewish Youth Camp
5540 Szarvas, Erzsébet liget
Tel.: +36 66 311 099,
Tel./Fax: +36 66 313 161
E-mail: jorge@jdc.hu, taly@jdc.hu, mircea@jdc.hu
Homepage: www.camp.jdc.hu

3.

The Jewish Museum and Archives of Hungary
1075 Budapest, 2 Dohány Street
Tel.: +36 1 342 8949
E-mail: bpjewmus@c3.hu
Homepage: www.c3.hu/~bpjewmus
Director: Róbert B. Turán
Director of the Archives: Zsuzsa Toronyi

Holocaust Documentation Centre and Memorial Collection Public Endowment
1094 Budapest, 39 Páva Street
Tel.: +36 1 216 6557
Fax: +36 1 215 3888
E-mail: iroda@bphm.org
Director: Dr. András Darányi

4.

Bálint Jewish Community Centre
1065 Budapest, Révay Street 16
Tel.: +36 1 311 9214, +36 1 311 6669, +36 1 353 4717
E-mail: info@jcc.hu
Homepage: www.jcc.hu
Director: Miklós Fischer

Makkabi Publishing Ltd.
1077 Budapest, 13 Wesselényi Street
Tel.: +36 1 267 8502
Editorial office: 1055 Budapest,
11 Szent István Boulevard

Tel.: +36 1 354 1560
Fax: +36 1 354 1561
E-mail: Makkabi@mail.tvnet.hu
Homepage: www.makkabi.hu, www.judaica.hu, www.zsido.hu

59.

Club of the Federation to Maintain Jewish Culture in Hungary (MAZSIKE)
1076 Budapest, 48 Garay Street
Tel.: +36 1 311 6665
E-mail: mazsike@freemail.hu
Homepage: www.mazsike.hu

JOURNALS AND PERIODICALS

Új Élet
1075 Budapest, 12 Síp Street
Tel.: +36 1 322 2829
Homepage: www.interdnet.hu/Zsido/ujelet.htm
Editor-in-Chief: Chief Rabbi Péter Kardos

The bi-weekly of the Alliance of the Jewish Congregations of Hungary.

Szombat
1065 Budapest, Révay Street 16.
Tel.: +36 1 311 6665
Fax: +36 1 311 6666
E-mail: szerkesztoseg@szombat.org

Homepage: www.szombat.org
Editor-in-Chief: Gábor T. Szántó

Journal of the Federation to Maintain Jewish Culture in Hungary, published ten times a year, with a special emphasis on community affairs and the arts.

Remény
1075 Budapest, 12 Síp Street
Tel.: +36 1 3421 335
Editor-in-Chief: István Gábor Benedek

Jewish periodical focusing on community life, literature and the arts.

Múlt és Jövő
1024 Budapest, 27 Keleti Károly Street
Tel./Fax: +36 1 316 7019, +36 1 438 3806
E-mail: mandj@multesjovo.hu
Homepage: www.multesjovo.hu
Editor-in-Chief: János Kőbányai

Jewish literature and arts journal.

Egység
1075 Budapest, 4 Wesselényi Street
Tel.: +36 1 268 0183
Homepage: www.zsido.com/magazines/egyseg
Editor: Baruch Oberlander

Periodical published by the Chabad Lubavits Jewish Education Association.

Erec
1062 Budapest, 5 Lovag Street
Tel.: +36 1 374 3065
Fax: +36 1 374 3071
E-mail: jafibp@ax.hu
Homepage: www.erec.hu
Editor-in-Chief: Péter Breuer

Monthly published jointly by the Zionist Federation of Hungary and the Jewish Agency of Budapest.

www.zsido.hu (Hungarian Jewish homepage)
1055 Budapest, 11 Szent István Boulevard
Tel.: +36 1 354 1560
Fax: +36 1 354 1561
E-mail: raj@zsido.hu
Editor-in-Chief: Rabbi Tamás Raj

SOCIAL INSTITUTION, NURSING HOMES

11.

Jewish Nursing Home
1145 Budapest, 53–55 Amerikai Road
Tel.: +36 1 251 5288
Director: Dr. Zsuzsa Deutsch

12.

Orthodox Jewish Nursing Home
1126 Budapest, 2/B Alma Street
Tel.: +36 1 355 2765
Director: Mrs Tibor Dickmann

13.

Újpest Nursing Home of the Budapest Jewish Community
1042 Budapest, 7 Liszt Ferenc Street
Tel.: +36 1 389 2536
E-mail: salom@interware.hu
Director: Mrs Róbert Deutsch
Director of the Special Unit: Katalin Torda

Holiday Resort of the Alliance of the Jewish Congregations of Hungary
8230 Balatonfüred, 6 Liszt Ferenc Street
Tel.: +36 87 313 404

RESTAURANTS, FOODSTORES, GIFT SHOPS

Jewish Tourism and Cultural Centre
Aviv Travel Trade 2000 Ltd.
(organiser of the Jewish Summer Festival)
1075 Budapest, 12 Síp Street
Tel.: +36 1 343 0420
Fax: +36 1 462 0478
E-mail: zsikk@axelero.hu
homepage: www. jewishfestival.hu
Director: Vera Vadas

49.

Biblical World Judaica Gallery

The Judaica, book and gift shop of the Makkabi Publishing Ltd.

(Several Judaica auctions are organised each year)

1075 Budapest, 13 Wesselényi Street

Tel.: +36 1 267 8502

Fax: +36 1 354 1561

E-mail: Makkabi@mail.tvnet.hu

Hompege: www.makkabi.hu, www.judaica.hu

King's Hotel and Restaurant (Glatt kosher)

1072 Budapest, 25–27 Nagydiófa Street

Tel.: +36 1 352 7675

Fax: ++36 1 352 7675

E-mail: kosherhotel@kosherhotel.hu

Homepage: www.kosherhotel.hu

Hanna Restaurant (Glatt kosher)

1074 Budapest, 35 Dob Street

Tel.: +36 1 342 1072

Café Noé

Jewish and diabetic cakes and sweets

1075 Budapest, 13 Wesselényi Street

Tel.: +36 1 344 4208

Fax: +36 1 354 1561

Homepage: www.torta.hu

Falafel Salad Bar
1061 Budapest, 53 Paulay Ede Street
Tel.: +36 1 267 9567

Fröhlich coffee-shop (kosher)
1074 Budapest, 22 Dob Street
Tel.: +36 1 267 2851

Carmel Cellar
1074 Budapest, 31 Dob Street
(entrance from Kazinczy Stret)
Tel.: +36 1 322 1834, +36 1 342 4585
Fax: +36 1 461 0024
E-mail: carmel@carmel.hu
Homepage: www.carmel.hu

Kinor David Restaurant (kosher)
1077 Budapest, 10 Dohány Street
Tel.: +36 1 413 7304
E-mail: kinordavid@hotmail.com

Restaurants in the provinces

Debrecen 4025, 26 Bajcsy-Zsilinszky Street
(Jewish community)
Tel.: +36 52 415 861
Butcher and bakery:
Debrecen 4025, 26 Bajcsy-Zsilinszky Street
Tel.: +36 52 415 861, +36 52 533 273

Miskolc 3225, 7 Kazinczy Street
(Jewish community)
Tel.: +36 46 344 884

Szeged 6722, 12 Jósika Street
(Jewish community)
Tel.: +36 62 423 849

Balatonfüred 8230, 6 Liszt Ferenc Street
(holiday resort)
Tel.: +36 87 343 404

Rothschild Kosher Foodstore
1074 Budapest, 12 Dob Street
Tel.: +36 1 267 5691

Kosher wine cellar
1072 Budapest, 16 Klauzál Square
Tel.: +36 1 322 6898

Orthodox Kosher poultry shop and bakery
1072 Budapest, 28 Kazinczy Street
Tel.: +36 1 342 0231

Ortodox kosher butcheries
1074 Budapest, 35 Dob Street
Tel.: +36 1 344 5165
1132 Budapest, 16 Visegrádi Street
Tel.: +36 1 320 4454

Kővári's sausage factory and shop
(Orthodox kosher)
1074 Budapest, 35 Dob Street
Tel.: +36 1 342 1639

6.

Ritual bath (mikveh)
1072 Budapest, Kazinczy Street 16
Tel.: +36 20 423 7320
Director: András Grisztel

The single ritual bath in Budapest that, conforming to Jewish and tradition, uses "living water" (i.e. water of natural origin and not tap water).

Burial monument of Alfréd Hajós in the Rákoskeresztúr cemetery

The crypt of the Schmidl family in the Rákoskeresztúr cemetery

Chevra Kadisha
1075 Budapest, 12 Síp Street
Tel.: +36 1 322 7246
Director: László Garami

Jewish cemeteries in Budapest
(Most cemeteries have a caretaker and can thus be visited between 8 a.m and 4 p.m.)

35.
Rákoskeresztúr cemetery
1108 Budapest, 6 Kozma Street
Tel.: +36 1 265 2458, +36 1 262 4687
Director: Gábor Karádi

36.
Orthodox cemetery
1106 Budapest, 12 Gránátos Street
Tel.: +36 30 258 3930

37.
Farkasrét Cemetery
1124 Budapest, 9 Érdi Road
Tel.: +36 1 249 2671

38.
Óbuda cemetery
1037 Budapest, 369 Külső Bécsi Road
Tel.: +36 1 250 6060

39.

Kerepesi cemetery
1186 Budapest, Salgótarjáni Road
Tel.: +36 1 314 1269

40.

Old Orthodox cemetery
1124 Budapest, 55 Csörsz Street
Tel.: +36 1 339 8395
Director: Béla Davidovics

Similarly to the no longer used Jewish cemetery in Prague, burials in this picturesque old cemetery ceased in 1961. (Visits can be arranged at the offices of the Autonomous Orthodox Community of Hungary at 35 Dob Street.)

Suggested walks and sightseeing tours

JEWISH SIGHTS AND MONUMENTS IN BUDAPEST

The Jewish community of Budapest is the largest in Central Europe. The overwhelming majority of Hungarian Jewry lives in Budapest.

The synagogue triagle (the former ghetto)

The first walk explores the old Jewish quarter of Budapest, starting from the Dohány Street Synagogue on Herzl Tivadar Square on the corner of Károly Boulevard and Wesselényi Street. The Jewish quarter evolved at the turn of the eighteenth and nineteenth centuries outside the town wall of Pest, along the road leading to the Danube crossing-place. The Jewish quarter lay near the one-time Újvásártér [New Market Square]; its core was the Orczy House, demolished in 1939, and Király Street. The Pest ghetto, one of whose gates lay by the arcade on Wesselényi Street, was set up in this quarter in 1944. Some seventy thousand people, stripped of their belongings and rights, living in constant fear of death, were crammed into this picturesque town quarter with its narrow streets. The greater part of the Jewish sights and monuments of Pest lie in this area. The Hungarian Jewish Museum, the synagogues and offices of the Neolog and Orthodox congregations too lie in this area. The sights and monuments include a number of still active synagogues, the Martyrs' cemetery, the memorials and memorial plaques of the victims of the Holocaust and the life-saving heroes, one-time and still active Jewish schools, and a number of kosher restaurants and kosher food stores, catering to the needs of observant Jews leading a traditional Jewish life.

Great Synagogue in Dohány Street

(2 Dohány Street. Opening times: Monday–Friday: 10 a.m. to 5 p.m., Sunday: 10 a.m. to 1 p.m. The entrance ticket to the Jewish Museum is also valid for the synagogue. Hungarian and foreign language guides are available on request.)

This synagogue is the second largest Jewish temple in the world. Built in the Moorish style, the building was designed by the German architect Ludwig Förster, who also prepared the plans for the Great Synagogue in Vienna. It was dedicated on September 6, 1859.

Owing to the building's eastern orientation, the façade diverges slightly from the street's direction. A Biblical quote in Hebrew is set above the façade: "And let them make me a sanctuary, that I may dwell among them" (Exodus 25: 8). The stone tablets atop the tympanum between the two 43.61 m high towers crowned by lovely, green domes with golden ornaments symbolize the Tablets of the Law.

Three double doors ornamented with decorative metal mounts lead to the synagogue's vestibule. The aula is topped by three domes, of which the central one is the largest. All three are painted with vivid motifs. This space is lit by the small rose window set above the middle portal.

The majestic main hall, the synagogue's main interior space, has a striking mosaic floor, whose vibrant, geometric motifs pulse with the same rhythm. The axis of the pews draws the eye to the *Aron Kodesh,* the 8.2 m high Holy Ark, the most important religious element. The ground floor was originally reserved for men, while women were relegated to the first and second floor gallery. (Since World War 2, however, women are also allowed to use the ground floor.)

The entire synagogue is ornamented with Oriental style frescoes, gilding, stained glass windows, elaborate chandeliers and beautifully carved benches. The three-nave monumental interior space with its three galleries is roofed with a wooden casemate ceiling painted with exuberant geometric patterns, resting on slender iron pillars. The wall is pierced by arched windows on the ground floor and the first storey, decorated with the six-pointed Star of David set against a blue background. Light streaks in through three large rose windows on the second storey, creating an intimate atmosphere. The imposing side-pulpit with its spiral steps is set beside the first pillars, reflecting a cultural impact from Catholicism. From this pulpit, the rabbi's voice could fill the huge synagogue.

The Great Synagogue in Dohány Street

Interior of the Great Synagogue

Opposite the main entrance, on the main eastern wall is the large, domed Ark (not unlike a separate temple within the building) for the Torah scrolls designed by Frigyes Feszl. Its doors are concealed by a velvet curtain and a tapestry, both embroidered with Hebrew words and Jewish symbols. Above the Ark, a quote from the Psalms reminds the congregation of the place's sanctity: "From the rising of the sun unto the going down of the same, the Lord's name is to be praised."

The area in front of the Ark, set on a few steps' high platform enclosed by a railing, is undoubtedly one of the synagogue's most attractive interior spaces with its variety of ornamental and structual elements, reflecting the influence of Frigyes Feszl, designer of the Pest Redout. The ornamental motifs, the choice of colours, the use of fine materials reflects his love of Oriental culture. The ornate railing is a magnificent masterpiece with delicate architectural proportions. The rabbi preached to his congregation on Friday evenings and Saturday mornings from the pulpit in the centre. The elaborately ornamented chairs were occupied by members of the congregation, who were honoured with holding the Torah scrolls removed from the Ark during the service on Saturday mornings. In the centre stands the ornate folding pulpit ornamented with wooden statues of the lions of Judah, which when folded serves as a reading desk for the Torah and the cantor's pulpit. The chairs reserved for the community leaders are set on either side.

Three steps lead to the rabbi's seat on the left and the cantor's seat on the right. Their back echoes the design of the Ark. Two slender lamps, each with fourteen bulbs, are set in front of the seats.

A few steps covered with Persian rugs lead to the Ark. The mosaic floor underneath these rugs is covered with intricate geometric patterns. The portal with two marble columns, surmounted with a slightly irregular tympanum, springs out from the plane of the Ark; in its centre is the tetragrammaton YHWH. The Ark is crowned with a dome (resembling the dome over the synagogue's main hall) topped with a Star of David. The curtains of the Ark date from different periods; most are embroidered with Biblical motifs, texts in Hebrew, the name of the donor and the date of the donation. In front of the Ark is the eternal light, the *ner tamid*.

The Torah mantles protecting the Torah scrolls are embroidered with the name of the donor and the date of the donation. The ornamental motifs include the lions of Judah, the Tablets of the Covenant and the Torah crown. The space above the Ark is lit by a seven branched menorah.

The area behind the Ark accomodates the rabbi's and cantor's changing-room, and the room of the bride and the groom. The wedding canopy, the *huppah*, is also kept here.

41. 43.

Martyrs' cemetery

The open plots beside the synagogue were built up between 1929 and 1933. When designing the small garden enclosed by the Great Synagogue, the museum, the arcades and the Martyrs' Temple, the aim was the creation of an elegant, carefully planned, uniform space harmonising with the synagogue. A row of arcades similar to the one on the street graces the wall of the synagogue. In 1944, the garden was used as a cemetery, where the victims of Fascist brutality, epidemics and famine were buried. Many were exhumed on the request of their family or relatives and re-buried elsewhere. The ashes of some seven thousand victims, however, still lie here. One end of the cemetery is bordered by the façade of the Heroes' Temple with its triple entrance, harmonising with the row of arcades. The walls of the cemetery towards Dohány Street bear lists commemorating the names of the Jewish soldiers fallen in the Great War and a recently erected Hannah Szenes memorial plaque. (Hannah Szenes emigrated to Palestine from Hungary; as a lieutenant of the British army, she was parachuted into the country with the task of organizing resistance against the Fascists. She was captured and executed.) The memorial plaque erected by the Fencing and Athletic Club and Hashomer Hatzair are also set here. In the centre of the U shaped cemetery section is the memorial of the Pest ghetto: a large piece of wood topped with barbed wire. This memorial was erected here because one of the ghetto's entrances stood beside the cemetery, in Wesselényi Street (its exact place is marked by a plaque on the wall.)

Several other memorial plaques can be seen on the walls of the cemetery, the Jewish Museum and the community's office building, including the one marking the place where Theodor Herzl's house once stood.

Hungarian Jewish Museum

(2 Dohány Street. Opening times: Monday-Thursday: 10 a.m. to 7 p.m., Friday: 10 a.m. to 2 p.m., Sunday: 10 a.m. to 2 p.m.)

The building next to the synagogue houses the Hungarian Jewish Museum. Theodor Herzl, the visionary of modern Israel, was born in the house that once stood on the same spot.

Designed by László Vágó and Ferenc Faragó, the museum was built in 1932 in the same style as the Great Synagogue to harmonise with its environment. The most valuable artworks and ritual objects in the museum collections were packed into crates and hidden in the basement of the Hungarian National Museum during the war. The museum was re-opened in 1947; in 1993, robbers broke into the museum and stole many precious artworks from the exhibition. These were later found and are now again exhibited.

A memorial plaque dedicated to Theodor Herzl, founder of political Zionism and visionary of the State of Israel, can be seen in the stairway.

A few gravestones from the Roman Age have been exhibited in front of the first hall. These are the earliest indications of Jewish presence in Hungary.

The first room has the Shabbat as its central theme. The central showcase holds Torah scrolls written on parchment, together with ornate Torah mantles, crowns and shields, as well as hand shaped Torah pointers (called *yad*). Surrounding the central case are other objects related to the Shabbat: Shabbat

Seder plate made from Herend porcelain
(Hungarian Jewish Museum)

Torah crown
(Hungarian Jewish Museum)

Hanukkia
(Hungarian Jewish Museum)

candlesticks, oil-lamps, cups and the finely wrought spice containers (*besamim* holders), candlesticks and colourful, braided candles used during the Havdalah, the ceremony performed at the end of the Shabbat. One interesting article is the so-called Shivisi tablet adorning the cantor's table, on which the minuscule letters of the Hebrew text, made using micrographical technique, form human figures (Solomon, David, Esther).

The second hall shows the world of festivities. The ritual objects used during Rosh Hashanah (the New Year) and Yom Kippur (the Day of Atonement) include the *shofar* made from ram's horn and the white robe, the *kittel*. The so-called high holidays are followed by the pilgrim holidays. The elaborately laid table for the Seder on the first and second eve of Pesach is one of the centrepieces. The showcases around the table contain the articles used during this ceremony: lavishly illustrated Haggadahs (the book recounting the exodus from Egypt read during the Seder), wine goblets, Seder plates (including magnificent pieces made from Herend porcelain), tiered matzah plates and ornate matzah covers.

Hanukkah is held in remembrance of the uprising led by the Maccabbees in 168 BCE. The eight (nine) branched candlesticks evoke the miracle in the Temple of Jerusalem. During Purim, the Biblical Book of Esther, recounting the miraculous deliverance of the Jews from their enemies, is read in the synagogue; it often written on a parchment scroll kept in an elaborately ornamented case. The tin Purim plates and rattles are also used during this festival.

The third room contains the artefacts of day to day life, a wide range of interesting, diverse objects used by observant, pious Jews from birth to death.

The last room is almost completely dark: it evokes the period of Fascism in chronological order, with heartbreaking photos, documents and object evoking sad memories.

Temporary exhibitions are held in the large halls on the second floor. These often include travelling exhibitions from foreign museums and the works of major Jewish painters, such as Chagall and Modigliani.

We continue our walk along Wesselényi Street.

42. □

Heroes' Temple

At the end of the arcades lining the cemetery in Wesselényi Street stands the gracefully proportioned, domed building with ornate parapet. Built on a square groundplan, the temple designed by László Vágó, Lajos Deli and Ferenc Faragó was built in 1931. Its name, Heroes' Temple, was given in commemoration of the Jewish soldiers of the Great War.

The Ark, covered with green marble, is set by the eastern wall *(mizrah)* opposite the entrance. The choir and the organ on the upper floor are separated from the synagogal space by a latticework screen with Star of David motifs. The temple is lit by two huge, stained glass windows in the form of a Star of David. A Hebrew inscription arranged into a Star of David motif above the entrance commemorates the soldiers fallen during World War 1. Two large menorahs flank the entrance. The reading desk for the Torah stands in front of the Ark.

The dome of the temple is decorated in the Orientalising style, with a stained glass window in the form of a Star of David in the centre. The menorah shaped wall-lamps are distinctive elements of the elegant internal furnishings, echoing the building's overall style.

44.

Raoul Wallenberg memorial garden

The secretary of the Swedish embassy made heroic efforts to save the persecuted Jews during the Holocaust – many thousands owe their life to him. At the end of the war, Wallenberg was arrested by the Russians and probably deported to the Gulag, where he perished. His memory is preserved by this garden, a street, several memorial plaques and a statue.

The Holocaust Memorial of the Emanuel Foundation is also set in this garden.

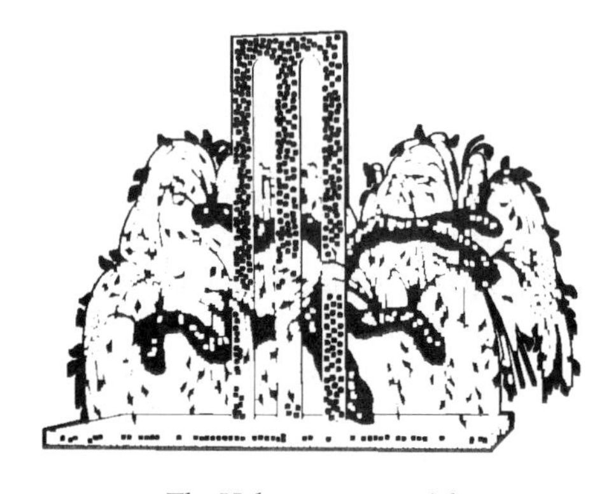

The Holocaust memorial

Wallenberg memorial (Budapest, Szilágyi Erzsébet fasor)

Each leaf of the metal willow-tree made by Imre Varga bears the name of a victim of the Holocaust. The memorial plaques of the Righteous Gentiles, who risked their own life to save others, have also been placed in the memorial garden. Many memorial plaques can be found in other parts of Budapest: the memorial plaque of the Papal legate, Monsignor Angelo Rotta has been placed on the wall of the house at 6 Úri Street (in the Castle District), while that of Giorgo Perlasca in the Szent István Park (district XIII).

50.

The Rumbach Sebestyén Street synagogue

(11–13 Rumbach Sebestyén Street)

Designed by Otto Wagner (the "father of Art Nouveau"), the second synagogue of the "synagogue triangle" was built in the Romantic Moorish style in 1872. This synagogue was the main Budapest synagogue of the so-called Status Quo (Conservative) movement, the second major religious movement of Hungarian Jewry. (This movement was called Staus Quo because unlike the Neolog or the Reform movement, they did not wish to introduce any reforms, but neither did they favour the strict measures advocated by the Orthodox; their position was summed up by the Latin phrase *status quo ante,* i.e. that all remain as before.) The building is no longer in the possession of the Jewish community; it is currently being renovated and therefore not open to visitors.

Orth

Orthodox Great Synagogue and offices

Approaching from Wesselényi Street, the third synagogue of the "triangle" in time-worn Kazinczy Street is visible from afar. In spite of the narrow street, its position allows an excellent view of this magnificent, Late Art Nouveau building. The main entrance is the most emphatic architectural element of the red brick façade. The synagogue can be entered by ascending four steps. The arched, two-winged main entrance has an emphatic frame and is flanked by two rectangular entrances. The doors were made from wrought iron decorated with a geometric pattern arranged

Façade of the Kazinczy Street synagogue

around a central Star of David. Above the gates are the arched windows of the first and second floor framed with elaborately carved stone, above which is set a round rose window with a Star of David motif. The façade is crowned with a lovely cresting, bearing a Biblical Hebrew quote on its middle and lower third: "This is none other, but the house of the Lord, and this is the gate of Heaven" (Genesis 28: 17).

The entrance to the Shas Chevra prayer-house can be found in gateway. The narrow, street-like courtyard beside the synagogue evokes the atmosphere of medieval ghettoes. In front of the rear façade is the platform for the *huppah,* the wedding canopy, with its fine, wrought iron railing, bearing a Hebrew inscription: "The voice of joy and the voice of gladness, the voice of the bridegroom and the voice of the bride" (Jeremiah 33: 11). The rear and the side façades are plain, without any ornamentation. The slender, elongated, arched stained glass windows are

The Orthodox synagogue in Kazinczy Street

decorated with a simple, geometric pattern and the occasional Star of David and the seven-branched menorah set in a circle.

A stairway leading to women's gallery on the first and second floor was built at each corner of the synagogue. The interior of the east oriented synagogue is three-naved, with two galleries. The costly and time-consuming renovation of the imposing building is nearly finished. Its internal furnishings are characterised by superb craftsmanship. The ceiling is pierced by widows with a delicate lacework pattern. The restoration of the colourful frescoes with flower motifs covering the walls are also nearing completion. The bell shaped bronze chandeliers, the carved benches and the desk on the large *bimah* with five steps in the centre of the synagogue are all beautifully crafted. The chief ornament of the synagogue is the Ark flanked by a pair of columns and half-columns on the eastern wall with a marble facing.

The winter prayer-house and the Orthodox kosher Hannah Restaurant both open from the courtyard. The offices of the Hungarian Autonomous Orthodox Jewish Community, whose main façade is on Dob Street, can also be accessed through the large, arched gate.

OTHER JEWISH SIGHTS AND MONUMENTS IN PEST

3.
Jewish Theological Seminary – University of Jewish Studies

(2 Bérkocsis Street)

The idea of creating a Rabbinical Seminary first took shape in the nineteenth century. The earliest modern rabbinical seminaries were founded in Metz (1829) and Padova (1830). In 1908, David Friedhausen, a scholar of Bavarian origin, suggested the establishment of a rabbinical seminary in Hungary.

A huge collective fine was imposed on the Jews of Hungary for their participation in the 1848–49 War of Independence; this sum was later used for the creation of a School Fund. The Rabbinical Seminary was eventually built from this fund. The National Rabbinical Seminary, named after Francis Joseph I, was opened on October 4, 1877, on the basis of a ministerial decree. A total of 320 rabbis have been ordained to date. Many Hungarian rabbis perished during the Holocaust, including eighty-nine of the rabbis ordained in the seminary, together with several students of the seminary.

Currently, the Jewish Theological Seminary and University of Jewish Studies offers three major courses (Rabbinical Studies, Liturgical History and Cantor Training), while the College has two main courses (Teacher Training for Judaic Studies and Jewish Community Social Work). Postgraduate courses on Jewish cultural history also are offered.

The Theological Seminary and University occupy two buildings. The four storey corner house at 27 József Boulevard was built in the late nineteenth century. It was donated to the Francis Joseph I Rabbinical Institute (as it was then called) by József Freund and his wife in 1918. The plaque commemorating the donors' name is set above the entrance. The offices of the College and of Dr. József Schweitzer, the retired Chief Rabbi, are located on the second floor of the building.

The other building is the two-storey, red brick school building on the corner of Bérkocsis and Somogyi Béla Streets that had originally been built for training rabbis and teachers. The one-time Jewish Teacher Training College occupied the ground floor and the first floor. The building's elegant proportions, its lovely façade ornamentation and large windows fit nicely into the architectural landscape of the Inner Józsefváros district. The building's corner faces Gutenberg Square. The harmony of the building incorporating many Orientalising architectural elements can be best appreciated if viewed from this square. The three corner pilasters, the facing and its ornamentation all highlight the building's architectural unity. The vibrant Orientalising ornamentation around the triple arched windows temper the austerity of the massive walls.

Entering the building, the eight memorial plaques set on the walls of the attractive, columned entrance hall draw the visitor's eyes. These commemorate the dedication of the seminary and various anniversaries, as well as the victims of the Holocaust from the Theological Seminary and the Gymnasium.

A staircase with fine wrought-iron railing leads from the aula to the upper floors. The corridors are decorated with old tableaus and memorial plaques.

The lecture halls, the library, the archives and other educational rooms lie in the street wing of the U shaped building. The courtyard wing accommodates the synagogue and the ceremonial hall of the Theological Seminary and the University.

The Rákoskeresztúr cemetery

(6 Kozma Street)

Hungary's largest Jewish cemetery can be reached by tram 37, whose end station is in Népszínház Street, not far from the Jewish Theological Seminary. The large, ornate funeral parlour, dedicated in 1891, can be seen from afar. The high central part of the tripartite building is decorated with large domes at the corners and a scalloped stucco ornamentation. The large, triple entrance and the arched windows beside it are set in the middle of the façade. The offices and the waiting rooms are in the building's side-wing. The inner façade, facing the cemetery, is likewise stuccoed with floral and shell motifs. The large, two-winged doors leading to the mortuaries open from this façade.

The central part of the building accommodates the "first-class" mortuary, while the "second-class" one is to its right. The large, "first-class" mortuary is painted with grey and white. Two large, bronze chandeliers with delicate ornamentation hang from the stuccoed ceiling. Above the dark brown doors are stained glass windows decorated with star motifs. The carved pulpit in front of the main wall is flanked by the benches for the family and close relatives, with the raised platform for the coffin surrounded by candelabrums in the centre. A carved wooden railing and four large menorahs accentuate the hall's sombre pomp. The mourners are seated in benches carved in the same style.

The "second-class" mortuary is a simple room with carved wooden benches. To the left of the funeral parlour are the *tahorah* rooms for the preparation of the deceased for burial. The large entrance hall lies in the part of the building facing the street, behind the no longer used main entrance. Memorial plaques and plaques commemorating the victims of the Holocaust have been set on the walls of the domed, stucco decorated hall, many of them brought here from demolished Jewish synagogues and other institutions. They include the plaques listing the victims of the Holocaust from the one-time Kőbánya, Jászapáti and Mezőtúr synagogues, as well as plaques commemorating the founders of the former Jewish apprentice home, hospice and hospital.

The cemetery can be entered through two gates. We shall begin the description of the cemetery from the pedestrian entrance. Facing the entrance is a pillar topped by a memorial lamp with the Tablets of the Law carved in stone. Opposite the funeral parlour is the memorial to the ten thousand Jewish soldiers fallen during the Great War, bearing the inscription "To the memory of the heroes fallen in the Great War". Near to it stands a simple memorial to the unknown members of the forced labour battalions.

By the car entrance stands the sad sight of the imposing Martyrs' Memorial. The memorial dedicated to the six hundred thousand Hungarian Jewish victims of the Holocaust is an L shaped monument enclosing the area to the left of the funeral parlour. Nine memorial walls inscribed with tens of thousands of names are set perpendicular to the longitudinal axis. In addition to the names of the people deported from various towns and villages, listed in alphabetical order, are the names of the families that were omitted from the original list, written in pencil.

The short "stem" of the L shaped memorial forms the towering main wall of the memorial, inscribed with the following text: "Though killed by hatred, may their memory be preserved by love." The plain, black marble slab in front of the wall is covered with flowers and wreaths. The memorial is guarded by a large menorah set into the wall.

In the memorial space enclosed by trees lie the martyrs' graves, into which were buried either single individuals or the members of an entire family, a village or a town (in many cases, the stones only preserve the victims' memory since many perished outside Hungary, in the gas chambers of Auschwitz). Among the memorials is one with the depiction of a large Torah scroll, a menorah and the Tablets of the Law, inscribed with the following text: "In memory of the 196 members of the 161/322 forced labour battalion who were murdered on their way home, on October 11, 1944, at Kiskunhalas."

The remains of damaged and desecrated Torah scrolls were buried in two graves behind this memorial. According to Jewish religious law, if the sacred scrolls become damaged, they can no longer be used and must be buried.

The parcels of the Holocaust victims (parcel A) beginning at the memorial contain rows upon rows of huge mass graves, arranged according to a uniform design created in 1945-46, into which the exhumed victims were laid to rest (they included the exhumed bodies from Balf, Lichtenworth, Sopronkőhida, Kőszeg, Klauzál Square in Budapest and from other places).

Near the Martyrs' Memorial lie the graves of the Jewish men and women, who were members of the resistance movement. A little farther away, grave 3/23 in plot 5/c contains the burial of Hannah Szenes, the British paratrooper lieutenant, a hero of the Zionist resistance movement. (Her body was exhumed in 1950 and the ashes were reburied in Israel; only the 2 m high column with the bronze plaques bearing military insignia remains.)

The graves of the rabbis, cantors and community leaders lie in plot 4/a, behind the Martyrs' Memorial. Chief Rabbi Simon Hevesi, one of the outstanding religious-spiritual leaders of Hungarian Jewry during the interwar years, is buried here, as is Chief Rabbi Dr. Sándor Scheiber, the renowned scholar and former director of the Jewish Theological Seminary, who died in 1985. A little farther away is the grave memorial of Izrael Tkatsch, the wonderful chief cantor of the Rumbach Street synagogue.

Opposite this plot are the oldest graves of the cemetery, relocated from the old Váci Road cemetery that ceased to be used in 1910. The first post-medieval Jewish cemetery in Pest was opened on Váci Road; when the use of this cemetery was discontinued in 1848, the Jewish community buried its dead on Lehel Road, near present-day Lehel Square. This cemetery was filled up in 1874, and was abandoned around the turn of the century. The prominent deceased were reburied in the then new cemetery.

At the corner of the plot and in the first row there are lovely box tombs inscribed in Hebrew. One of them is the grave of Simon Oppenheimer, a rabbi active in Pest, who died in 1851. His grave is a place of pilgrimage for his followers, who place slips of papers inscribed with their wishes into the cracks on the gravestone. The many stones placed on the grave were also left by pious visitors.

Two rabbis of the renowned Wahrmann family are also buried here: Juda Wahrmann, who was Chief Rabbi between 1796–1826, and his son Izrael Wahrmann, the first Chief Rabbi of Pest. (The latter's son, Mór Wahrmann, was the first Jewish member of

Hungarian Parliament, and president of the National Alliance of Industrialists.) Illés Adler, the renowned Chief Rabbi of the Rumbach Street synagogue and of the Status Quo congregation is likewise buried in this part of the cemetery under a grave decorated with an eagle. The rabbi who was renowned for his wonderful, inspiring sermons died in 1929. Near him lies the historian Sámuel Kohn (d. in 1920), who from 1866 acted as the rabbi and, later, as the Chief Rabbi of the Neolog congreation of Pest and of the Dohány Street synagogue. The acclaimed scholar was one of the most ardent protagonists of the Magyarisation of the Jews of Hungary.

In the corner of plot 4/A lie the burials of the Jewish soldiers of the 1848–49 War of Independence and of the composer Márk Rózsavölgyi.

Plot 5/b contains the burials of well known artists and scholars, the eminent representatives of twentieth century Hungarian-Jewish intellectuals. They include the graves of historians Henrik Marczali and Ignác Kunos, the journalist Miksa Szabolcsi, the novelists Sándor Bródy, István Szomaházay, Tamás Kóbor and Ernő Szép, the opera singer Oszkár Kálmán, the actor Gyula Bartos, the surgeon Dr. Jónás Báron, all of whom lived during the interwar period.

Many graves of outstanding persons who died more recently stand out by their unusual form. One good example is the grave of the opera singer Árpád Kishegyi, marked with a modern tombstone crowned with an iron menorah, erected in 1989; another is the gravestone carved from a single block of stone, marking the burial of the mining engineer and scholar Dr. István Gaál. Lipót Hermann's name is inscribed with lead letters embedded into an unhewn block of stone. The actor Gyula Gózon's grave is covered with a mantle crafted from iron. The burials of Noémi Kóbor and Adorján Stella lie beside each other. Dezső Kellér's gravestone has a bronze relief depicting a hand holding theatre curtains, while Andor Kellér's takes the form of a theatre box.

On the right of the cemetery's main path stands the burial of Alfréd Hajós, the first Olympic champion of Hungary. The crypt is decorated with the five Olympic circles.

Before leaving the cemetery, it is worthwhile to stroll to the row of crypts along the cemetery wall. Starting from the main building, the second crypt to the right is the one belonging to the Brüll family. The walls and the ceiling of the crypt designed by Alajos Stróbl are covered with a colourful mosaic; a huge vase is set into the niche, the crypt itself is flanked by lions. (Alfréd Brüll, the renowned leader and patron of the MTK Sports Club, was a member of this family.) Another noteworthy grave memorial is the magnificent Art Nouveau crypt containing the burial of Sándor Schmidl, adorned with green, blue and gold majolica flowers, its interior covered with a mosaic of vibrant colours. Above the gold mosaic covering the entrance is a blooming fruit tree, while the walls are ornamented with flowers.

Jewish sights and monuments in Buda

A number of remarkable Jewish monuments can be found near Bécsi-kapu Square in the Castle District (it can be reached by taking the castle bus from Moszkva or Deák Square).

102.

Medieval Jewish synagogue in Buda Castle

(26 Táncsics Mihály Street; open in summer only. Opening times: Tuesday–Friday: 10 a.m. to 3 p.m., Saturday-Sunday: 10 a.m. to 6 p.m.)

The medieval synagogue in Buda was discovered in 1964, during the excavations in the Castle District. The building housing the museum on the opposite side of the street had once belonged to Jakab Mendel, the Jewish Prefect. In 1482, King Matthias appointed him to this post, earlier held by a Christian noble. He and his descendants collected the Jewish tax and managed the Jewish community's affairs. During the Ottoman period, the building was transformed into a Sephardic prayer-house. Today it accommodates a Jewish museum and a collection of Jewish gravestones. Above the entrance is a Cabbalistic inscription in red from the later seventeenth century.

A memorial plaque on the wall of the Evangelical church beside the museum is dedicated to the pastor Gábor Sztehlo, who saved hundreds of Jewish children during the Holocaust.

On the other side of the street stood the medieval great synagogue, whose walls were reburied after the conclusion of the excavations.

The Jewish cemetery of Buda, established in 1885, can be reached by taking tram 59 from Moszkva Square, a short walk from the medieval synagogue.

Farkasrét cemetery

(9 Érdi Road; open daily: 8 a.m. to 4 p.m.)

The street façade of the simple, red brick funeral parlour is unadorned, except for the three arched blind windows and the round window above them in the central, higher part of the building. The wall beside the large glass doors leading to the mortuary is covered with memorial plaques of World War 1. The podium for the coffin, flanked by candelabra, is set in the centre of the plain, rectangular room. In front of the podium is the rabbi's pulpit, flanked by benches. The ceiling of the austere room has a single Star of David in its centre and menorahs in its corners. Six wall-lamps are set on the walls.

In front of the building lie the burials of the one-time rabbis of the Buda congregation. These include the graves of Rafael Goldberg (d. 1900) and Arnold Kiss (who wrote the women's prayer-book still used today), as well as of Artúr Gerey and Imre Benoschofsky, the two influential rabbis of the post-war period. Near them lies Bernát Heller, who taught Bible at the Jewish Theological Seminary and who was the first director of the Jewish gymnasium of Budapest.

Many illustrious persons are buried in this cemetery. Walking from the funeral parlour, the burials along the path by the outer wall include the grave of the gunmaker Rudolf Frommer, designer of the renowned Frommer pistols. Next to his burial, an unpretentious, practically undecorated black marble column marks the grave of architect László Dános. Another renowned architect, László Vágó is also buried here. The reliefs on his gravestone depict some of the buildings designed by him, such as the Heroes' Temple in Wesselényi Street. The poet Lajos Palágyi and Dr. Sándor Ferenczy, founder of the Hungarian psychoanalytical school, were also laid to rest here. One interesting section of this burial ground is the military parcel, where the Jewish soldiers fallen in the Great War were buried under identical gravestones inscribed with the text *Pro patria.* As customary among soldiers, the first burial in this section is the grave of the highest-ranking offier, General Gyula Krupieci Bauer, commander of the famous "What the deuce?!" regiment. Dr. Gyula Kepes, the single Hungarian member of the 1872–73 expedition to the North Pole, Kornél Lánczos, an atomic scientist, lecturer of the Royal Irish Academy, the painter Miklós Farkasházy and composer János Hammerschlag are all interred here. Grave monuments from different periods made in a variety of styles lie beside each other, ranging from the simple, worn tombstones of the 1850s to gravestones reflecting the different artistic styles of the 1930s and modern, tasteful grave monuments of our own age. The language of the inscriptions on the gravestones varied from period to period: Hebrew, German, and Hungarian texts can be found in each other's vicinity.

40.

Old Orthodox cemetery

(55 Csörsz Street)

One of the oldest Jewish cemeteries in Budapest is wedged in-between modern houses and factories. Approaching from the street, one first sees the red tiled roof of a white walled building lying well below the modern pavement level: the one-time mortuary, which is currently the caretaker's lodge. A simple plaque by the entrance lists the names of the many people who helped the renovation of this burial ground.

A path leads through the roughly 100 m long and 10 m wide cemetery. On both sides, the older and newer, plain and more elaborate gravestones lie in picturesque, unruly groups, often atop each other.

This burial ground resembles the famous Old Jewish cemetery in Prague. Since this is an Orthodox burial ground, the tombstones are all inscribed in Hebrew and bear traditional motifs, such as the priestly hand raised in benediction (a Cohanite symbol), the pitcher (a symbol of the Levites), and the weeping willow, as well as the occasional coat-of-arms. Many gravestones are damaged, have fallen or are pockmarked with bullet marks. The last burial took place in 1961, after which the cemetery was closed down.

Near the mortuary, beside the path lies the grave of Koppel Reich, the Orthodox Chief Rabbi. He was elected rabbi of the Budapest Orthodox congregation in 1890 and later rose to become its Chief Rabbi. The Orthodox community became strong and well organised under his spiritual leadership. Behind the large gravestone topped with a carved crown is a tent shaped stone chest with openings for the *kvittel* (the small slips of paper with a request written on them) brought by his followers. Near him lies his son-in-law, Hajim David Sofer (Schreiber), a descendant of the famous Moses Sofer (the Hatam Sofer) of Bratislava. According to the family tradition, Moses Sofer was a descendant of Rashi, the distinguished Bible commentator of the eleventh century. The family gave many illustrious rabbis to Jewish scholarship. The family's name is telling: the word *sofer* means Torah scribe or simply a literate person.

The miracle-working rabbi *(tzaddik)* of Akninitch (Galicia) too lies buried in this cemetery. He fled to Hungary during World War 1, to escape the bloodshed and the persecution of the Jews. He was supported by Jakab Schmutz, one of his disciples, who organised the rebbe's burial and who was in turn buried at the rebbe's feet. The rebbe's grave is still visited by many people.

The gravestone evoking the most tragic memories is the memorial to the doctors and the patients of the Jewish hospital in Maros Street and of the Bíró Dániel Orthodox Jewish hospital in Városmajor Street, who were brutally murdered by Arrow-Cross men. During the Holocaust, when the Jews of Buda and Pest were not allowed to leave the city's inner territory, they were allowed to bury their dead in this cemetery only until the ghetto was enclosed with a wall.

Near the entrance of the cemetery lie the burials of the Freudiger family of Óbuda. Mózes Freudiger, one of the founders of the textile industry in Óbuda, and later his sons played an important role in organising the Budapest Orthodox community as its secular leaders.

In the corner of the cemetery behind the mortuary lies another noteworthy memorial, a double tombstone of unusual form, marking the grave of a couple. The husband's tombstone bears a Cohanite hand raised in benediction, the wife's a heart.

The next town quarter with Jewish monuments lies by the Danube.

Óbuda

Jews settled in Óbuda, an originally independent town, by the fourteenth century; the first record documenting their presence dates from 1349. An influential, populous and privileged Jewish community emerged here in the eighteenth century. (Present-day Lajos Street was originally called Zsidó [Jewish] Street.) The Jews lived under the protection of the Count Zichy family; in exchange for the payment of an annual protection tax, the authorities did not harass them. The Zichys granted them various privileges. They were allowed to hold public services, to have their own judges for their internal affairs, to purchase real estate and to sell kosher meat and wine. The Jewish judge, whom the Jews of Óbuda elected from among themselves with the Zichys' permission, was held in great respect. The judge held an ornate silver cane in his hand, and when he walked the street, the beadle went before him. As leaseholders, the Jews lived scattered throughout the town. In 1737, there were forty-three families. They bought a piece of land for a cemetery at this time and they also built a synagogue. In 1770, the Chevra Kadisha, the holy brotherhood, an association for burial and charitable activities was founded. The public elementary school, the first secular Jewish school, was opened in 1784. By 1787, there were over three hundred Jewish families living in Óbuda. Many of them founded factories and a variety of workshops. One of these workshops, making white-patterned blue textiles (a fabric retaining its popularity ever since) was founded in 1784 by Ferenc Goldberg, a goldsmith. Originally called Perez, the Goldberg family's ancestors came from Spain, settling in Óbuda in the early eighteenth century. Ferenc Goldberg's son, Sámuel Goldberg was one of the pioneers of Hungarian industry – he was the founder of the Goldberger factory.

The Óbuda congregation is no longer an independent one: its members belong to the Buda District and neither do they have their own synagogue. With the exception of the one-time synagogue, most of the former Jewish institutions were demolished together with the other old houses of Óbuda.

114. ✳ ✎ 🏛 ◎

Former Óbuda synagogue

The first synagogue was built between 1767–69 according to the plans of Máté Nepauer. However, owing to the unfavourable soil conditions, its walls became cracked and the synagogue had to be rebuilt. Most of the walls have survived intact. (An architectural survey conducted in 1947 revealed that the synagogue's foundation walls rested on Roman remains.) A new southern façade, a portico and a new roofing was built. The building's exterior has remained unchanged since then: the building is mentioned in most descriptions of Budapest and appears in the townscapes from the nineteenth century to the present. Rebuilt according to András Landherr's design, the synagogue was consecrated in 1821. Its rabbi at the time was the famed Mózes Müncz (1750–1831).

Built in the Classicist style, the building's most attractive feature is the open portico with a tympanum supported by six Corinthian columns. Its groundplan measures 20.99 m by 34.07 m; its cornice rises at 13.2 m. Architecturally, the building resembles an incomplete basilica since the division of its interior space is asymmetrical. Aside from the rear gallery, only the northern side has a gallery. The synagogue's imposing dimensions, its huge dome, the architecture of the galleries and the fine craftsmanship of the *bimah* (the podium where the Torah is read) counterbalances the clumsiness of the asymmetric entrance. Its interior was also unique: the *bimah* in the centre was enclosed by four ornate columns. Synagogues of this type can be seen in Slovakia and at Apostag, a town on the Danube. The Jewish community sold the building in the 1960s, and it currently functions as a studio of Hungarian Television. The building's exterior has been preserved in its original form, while its interior has been transformed to correspond to its new function.

The grave of Mózes Müncz, the renowned Chief Rabbi of Óbuda, is a place of pilgrimage. He was buried in the picturesque Óbuda cemetery (369 Külső Bécsi Road). The cemetery is well worth a visit. Many painters draw inspiration from the cemetery even today: István Dési Huber painted several pictures of the cemetery.

A number of other Jewish sights and monuments can be found in Budapest. These are marked on the map with numerals, with their designation and exact address listed in the margin.

Jewish sights and monuments in the provinces

Up to World War 2, before the Holocaust, there were Jews in almost every village and town of Hungary. These Jewish communities built several hundred synagogues, and each had its own cemetery, school and other buildings. The greatest losses were suffered by provincial Jewry: of the several hundred thousand Jews, only a few thousand survived the Holocaust. The most important villages and towns, where relics of this Jewish past and still active institutions of modern Jewish life can be found, have been included in the suggested itineraries for visitors interested in the Jewish heritage of Hungary.

This section is divided into three parts. The first covers Transdanubia, the country's southern and western regions, where the monuments of medieval Jewish life have survived in some places. The second is the Great Hungarian Plain, where the Jews were proud to identify themselves as Hungarians and had strong national loyalties – synagogue sermons in Hungarian were first held in this region. The third part covers northern and northeastern Hungary, a region rich in Hassidic traditions.

Western Hungary

Starting from Budapest, we take Motorway M1 to Győr, the first stop on our itinerary.

Győr

Lying some 120 km from Budapest, the monumental synagogue built in the Romantic style (5 Kossuth Lajos Street) is a distinctive element of the townscape. The synagogue's large central dome can be seen from afar. The synagogue and the school buildings adjoining it are in state property; they are badly in need of renovation and for the determination of their possible new function.

We continue our journey along Road 85 to Sopron.

Sopron

The town on the western, Austrian border is one of Hungary's most popular tourist attractions. Visitors interested in Jewish architecture will find several fascinating monuments: two intact medieval synagogues, excavated by professional archaeologists, and the former medieval Jewish quarter.

It is believed that Jews first settled in this town during the Roman Age and that their presence was unbroken since the successive waves of the Migration period bypassed the town. Be as it may, there were several Jewish families in Sopron by the early fourteenth century. Their residence in Sopron was guaranteed by King Charles Robert in 1324. The 1379 land registry shows that twenty-seven houses were owned by Jews. By the sixteenth century there were some four hundred in Jews in the town, who had their own houses, synagogues and cemeteries.

As "servants of the Royal Chamber," the Jews enjoyed royal protection; the town's German burghers regarded them as serious competitors. Taking advantage of the troubled times after the Battle of Mohács and the death of King Louis II in 1526, the German burghers wanted to rid themselves both of the Jews and of their debts. They reasoned that if the Jews perhaps moved to another town, but took the promissory notes with them, the debts would have to be paid. Sensing an imminent pogrom, some of Sopron's Jewish inhabitants fled to Kismarton – they were ordered to return and were accused of being disloyal to the state. In early September, the Jews were told that they had one hour to leave the town or else they would be put to the sword. They were not allowed to take their belongings and they had to surrender the keys to their houses. After the expulsion of the Jews, their houses were ransacked, their synagogues were plundered and the promissory notes were destroyed. According to local tradition, there was a nailed-up gate called Blind Gate *(Blindes Tor)* near St. Michael's Gate. This gate was apparently nailed up after the expulsion of the Jews, an act symbolising that those who had departed through this gate should never return.

The Jews waged a long legal battle against the town, lasting for several centuries. In 1840, a decree of the Hungarian Diet allowed Jews to settle in the free royal towns and the Jews returned to Sopron. Most arrived from the so-called "Seven Communities" of Burgenland: Lakompak, Kis-Marton, Kabold, Köpcsény, Német-Keresztúr, Nagy-Marton and Boldogasszony, to where their ancestors had moved after being driven out of Sopron in 1526.

The Jews lived in their own street in the fourteenth century (the Judengasse [Jewish Street], present-day Új Street), where visitors find an almost intactly preserved medieval Jewish quarter. The Jewish quarter of Sopron rivals the one in Prague as regards its beauty and atmosphere.

Most houses in Új Street date from the Middle Ages; many preserve a number of Gothic elements.

The medieval synagogue at 11 Új Street was built around 1370, and was originally the private synagogue of a banker called Israel. When the Jews were driven out of Sopron, the prayer-house was transformed into a residential building. Its original function was forgotten. The building was discovered in 1957 by the architects of the National Monuments Board. Its conservation and renovation was completed in 1960.

Entering the courtyard, we find a Gothic stone door-frame to the left, the entrance of the one-time Jewish hospital. The red marble curb of the well of the ritual bath lies beside the wall on the right. Another stone-framed Gothic door leads to the vaulted exhibition hall on the street front. Passing through a vestibule, the visitor can enter the one-time synagogue. To the left of the entrance is a window, through which the women could watch the service from their own hall. The two-storey synagogue was lit by a pair of two stone-grated, Gothic windows (now walled up). The niche for the Ark was recessed into the eastern wall.

The medieval Old Synagogue stands on the opposite side of the street (22–24 Új Street). The first synagogue of the medieval Jewish community of Sopron was erected between 1300–1320. According to the medieval regulations, it was forbidden to build a synagogue in line with the street; jurisdiction and business deals with Gentiles were conducted in the courtyard, enclosed by a fence. Although the synagogue complex was transformed into a Baroque house after the expulsion of the Jews, the locals preserved the memory of this synagogue up to the end of the nineteenth century. The excavations begun in 1967 and the reconstruction work in 1974–75 enriched Sopron with magnificent and unique medieval monuments.

The street façade is formed by two buildings linked by a gate. The courtyard of the synagogue can be entered through an early eighteenth century arched gate. To the left stands the house of the Jew Joseph, restored in its original Baroque form. Across the entrance are the Gothic walls of the synagogue, its façade pierced by a stone mullioned rose window set between two narrow, arched windows. To the right stands the one-time hospice. The prayer room, the women's room and the ritual bath can be approached through a medieval corridor.

The two-storey high hall can be entered through a splayed Gothic door. Only the corbels and the springers of the cross-vault have survived; the current ceiling preserves no vestiges of the one-time vaulting. The excavations have brought to light the hexagonal foundation of the raised platform with the desk from which the Torah was read (the *almemor* or *bimah,* now covered with a modern, wooden superstructure). The niche in the eastern wall for the Ark is framed by Gothic tracery and carved grapevine motifs, on which remains of the original painting have survived. The steps leading to the niche and sections of the original flooring can be seen in front of the niche.

The windows of the women's prayer-room can be seen high up on the western wall. This closed gallery can be accessed from the corridor. An exhibition covering the history of Sopron's medieval Jewish community can be viewed in the gallery.

A splayed Gothic gate leads from the corridor to the synagogue's western courtyard and the ritual bath. The rectangular well, measuring 1.5 m by 1.5 m, was 4.2 m deep. The ladder of the well was also brought to light during the archaeological investigations. A domed protective building has been raised over the well, in which a part of the finds are now displayed.

Not far from the synagogue, in 5 Fegyvertár Street, lies the one-time Jewish school, where Miksa Pollák, the famed rabbi of Sopron and the historian of the Sopron community lived. His son, the renowned novelist Károly Pap, who perished in the Holocaust, spent his childhood here.

The walled cemetery lies in Tómalom Street on the edge of the town. In addition to the memorial of the Sopron Jews who perished in the Holocaust, memorials to the victims from Balf, Kópháza and Lichtenwörth have also been raised in the cemetery. (Contact person: Péter Keszthelyi, appointed leader of the community; Postal address: 9401 Sopron, Pf. 345.)

Kőszeg

In 1393, King Sigismund permitted the aristocratic Gara family to settle Jews in this town on the western, Austrian border. The Jewish community was dissolved and re-organised repeatedly as times changed. In 1526, after the Battle of Mohács, the Jews of Kőszeg were banished from the town, similarly to the Jews of Sopron. The Jews fled to Rohonc (present-day Rechnitz in Austria) on the estate of the Count Batthyány family. In spite of their persecution, Jewish suppliers helped Miklós Jurisich defend the Kőszeg fortress against the Turkish onslaught in 1532. The Jews were finally allowed to return in 1840. Today, there are hardly any Jews left in the town.

One interesting sight in the town's surviving medieval quarter is the dilapidated synagogue (41 Várkör). The synagogue was built in 1859 in the Romantic style; it has a roughly circular groundplan with three apses, an entrance flanked by two towers and a dome pierced by a round window. This remarkable, unique building is a listed monument, badly in need of conservation and renovation work.

Szombathely

Jews first settled in Szombathely in the earlier nineteenth century, at a time when both the town and the

Jewish community enjoyed a period of spectacular development. In 1941, the town's Jewish population numbered 3113; there was a separate Neolog and Orthodox congregation, each with its own synagogue, a school, a nursing home, an office building and several other institutions.

There is still an active congregation and a dynamic religious and community life. The building of the synagogue at 3 Rákóczi Ferenc Street (now a music school and concert hall) can be seen from afar in the Ruins Garden, where the remains of the Roman Age Isis sanctuary are displayed. Built in the Romantic style, the synagogue has two massive towers topped with openwork onion domes. The pilasters and the raised part above the Ark are topped with smaller onion domes. The building is decorated with lovely windows, a decorative cornice, and with colourful brickwork. The entrance was rebuilt rather tastelessly and a smaller wing was added to the northern side. The large memorial to the victims of the Holocaust has been erected on the building's southern side. The single-storey building at 9 Battyhyány Square behind the synagogue houses the community offices, as well as a prayer hall and a culture hall.

Pápa

The Jewish community was founded in 1749, with the support of Count Pál Esterházy. At first, the community supported the Reform movement; Rabbi E. W. Rappaport was the first to hold religious services in Hungarian in the country. On his suggestion Lipót Löw, earlier the rabbi of Nagykanizsa, became his successor in 1844. Rabbi Löw, who served as chaplain during the 1848-49 War of Independence, consecrated the great synagogue, which is now in bad need of renovation. During the War of Independence, he held a thanksgiving service in the synagogue. The greater part of the Pápa community later joined the Orthodox movement. Over three thousand Jews lived in Pápa before the war, most of whom perished in the Holocaust.

The remnants of this historical community now mostly live in the United States, where they form a strong, thriving Hassidic community. Their rabbi bears the title "Rabbi of Pápa" and together with his followers, he visits the town each year to evoke the memory of the ancestors and to remember the victims of the Holocaust. The imposing synagogue, built in the Classicist style in 1846, lies in Petőfi Street; the old and the new cemetery (in which the Holocaust memorial was erected) can be found on the road to Városlőd.

The Balaton region

We leave Budapest on Motorway M7. Our first stop is one of the most popular bathing resorts.

Siófok

The town underwent a dynamic growth after the construction of the Balaton railway line in 1860, and the Jewish community played an active role in turning the town into a major trade centre. Many renowned

Jewish writers and artists from Budapest bought a summer house in Siófok, including the writer Frigyes Karinthy and the actor Béla Salamon. Imre Kálmán, the acclaimed operetta composer, was born here.

The first post-war synagogue was built in Siófok in 1985, after the demolition of the old synagogue (built in 1869). The modern building at the corner of Budai Nagy Antal Street and Széchenyi Street serves the many visitors arriving here in summer. The exhibition in the Kálmán Imre Museum includes several Jewish exhibits (5 Kálmán Imre Promenade. Opening times: April 1–October 31: 9 a.m.–5 p.m., November 1–March 31: 10 a.m.–4 p.m., closed Mondays).

Road 71 takes us to Keszthely, one of the oldest Jewish centres in this region.

Keszthely

The community was founded by the Jews who settled on the estates of the Count Festetich family in 1766. One of the centres of Jewish activities was the so-called Pethő House (22 Kossuth Lajos Street), a medieval house rebuilt in the Baroque style with an arcaded façade. The renowned composer Károly Goldmark, son of the synagogue's then cantor, was born here on May 18, 1830.

The synagogue in the courtyard was built in 1852; the Classicist building was rebuilt in the Eclectic style in 1894. In accordance with the ancestral precepts, the synagogue was built slightly lower than the street level. Its interior is encircled by the women's gallery resting on wrought iron columns on three sides. The original Classicist architecture is preserved on the side façade and the eastern wall. The synagogue was recently renovated. The memorial to the victims of the Holocaust was erected by the entrance, while plaques bearing the names of the deceased were set on the walls inside the synagogue. Sándor Büchner, the community's rabbi, was a well-known historian, a privat-docent of Budapest University, who also died in the Holocaust.

Beside the synagogue are the winter prayer hall and the community offices. The building of the Transdanubian Talmud-Torah Centre at 1 Pető Street is owned by the community, which often organises cultural and educational programmes, as well as various exhibitions. The well-tended cemetery is in Goldmark Károly Street.

One interesting sight in the park behind the synagogue is the Bible Garden, opened in the summer of 2003, where unique plants from the Holy Land are exhibited. The garden was created with the generous help of the Helikon Castle.

A memorial to the victims of the Holocaust was erected in 2000 on the spot of the one-time synagogue near the entrance to the famed spa in nearby Hévíz, where annual commemorations are held for the deported Jews, whose ranks included Dr. Vilmos Schulhof, founder of the spa.

Balatonfüred

Continuing along Road 71, our next stop is Balatonfüred, where József Östereicher-Manes (1756–1832), the first Hungarian Jewish physician to graduate from university, founded the still active sanatorium, famed for its medicinal springs. Not far from the fountain lies the holiday resort of the Alliance of the Jewish Congregations of Hungary (6 Liszt Ferenc Street). Kosher meals can be obtained here by arrangement. The synagogue of the holiday resort is also open to visitors staying elsewhere.

Lovasberény

One of the oldest and most picturesque rural Jewish cemeteries can be found on the road to Vértesacsa.

Southern Hungary

For our third excursion to Transdanubia, we take Road 6 from Budapest.

Szekszárd

A larger Jewish community evolved in this town in the later nineteenth century. By 1910, the community numbered 840. The Jews built their own synagogue, a school, a rabbi's house, a ritual bath and they had their own butchery. Today, there are but a few Jews left – the memory of the one-time, flourishing community is preserved in the well-kept, walled cemetery, the synagogue (now transformed into a cultural centre and exhibition hall), the commemorative plaques and the memorial to the victims of Fascism.

The former synagogue, a finely renovated, impressive building, lies in the town centre near the Béri Balogh Ádám Museum on Szent István Square. Its façade has polygonal pilasters set on high bases that end in line with the ornate cornice, above which domed towers crown the building. The harmony of the building is enhanced by the rhythmic alternation of dark and light brick courses and the stone windows of varying sizes. The Tablets of the Law are set atop the central pilaster of the main façade.

Although the synagogue's interior has been redesigned according to its new function as an art gallery, the beauty of the original temple can still be felt.

Pécs

There was a flourishing Jewish community in Pécs during the Ottoman period; following the expulsion of the Turks, however, Jews were refused settlement in the town for a long time and were only allowed to do so after a bitter struggle for this right. Led by Bishop Radonay, the burghers of Pécs swore an oath on Easter Monday, 1692, that they would never allow non-Catholics to settle in their town and they renewed this oath each year.

The Edict of Tolerance issued by Joseph II did not soften the town councillors' hearts, even though Count Ferenc Széchényi, the royal commissioner (István Széchenyi's father) did everything he could to enforce the royal edict.

In spite of these difficulties, the Jewish community grew. In 1827, the Jews bought land for a cemetery and in 1843 they established a prayer-house in the

Engel House (10 Zrínyi Street). In 1843, a synagogue was built in Citrom Street. In 1849, Haynau imposed a collective fine of five thousand gold florins on the Jews for supporting the War of Independence.

The Jewish community underwent a period of dynamic growth in the later nineteenth century: the synagogue, still standing today, was built in 1868 and the other institutions of Jewish life, including the famous Jewish school, were also established. The community had several renowned rabbis, such as Sándor Kohut, Ármin Perls, Zoltán Wallenstein and József Schweitzer. Prominent members of the community included Lipót Fejér, the eminent mathematician, and the opera singer Dezső Ernster.

Pécs had a Jewish population of over three thousand before the war; ninety per cent perished in the Holocaust.

The great synagogue on Kossuth Square was designed by Károly Gerstner and Lajos Frey. Measuring 23.36 m by 32.35 m, the synagogue was built in the Romantic style. The façade is divided into three parts and three steps lead to the entrance. The arched central part rises above the roof-ridge; a clock was set in its centre, encircled by a Hebrew text: "For mine house shall be called a house of prayer for all people" (Isaiah 56: 7). The date of construction is indicated by the numerical value of the Hebrew letters. The pilasters are crowned with three onion dome-like ornaments; there are two large windows on top of the main arched façade and five windows on the side façades. A memorial plaque dedicated to the Jewish soldiers of the Great War has been set on the synagogue's wall.

The central triple doorway and a vestibule, whose walls are covered with memorial plaques, lead into the synagogue's main hall. The desk from which the Torah is read is set on the *mizrah* podium, separated from the rest of the hall by an ornate railing, between the pulpit and the Ark. The two columns flanking the Ark are connected with an arch and a dome surmounts the straight upper part of the Ark – the rays of the setting sun streaking in through the window often play on the dome. The letters on the floor in front of the desk record date of construction.

The two-storey women's gallery is supported by cast iron columns. The *mizrah* podium is flanked by the choir on one side and by the gallery of the organ, made by the Angster company of Pécs, on the other. The painted decoration and interior furnishings of the synagogue enhance its beauty. The memorial plaque of the Jewish soldiers of the Great War is set on the wall. The finely renovated synagogue is one of the main attractions of Pécs.

The renovated office building of the Jewish community lies near the synagogue (11 Fürdő Street). The building accommodates the rabbi's and the cantor's flat and the various community offices. In the courtyard stands the winter synagogue, where religious services are held regularly. Its unpretentious interior furnishings reflect a taste for tradition. The culture hall, the setting for community events and festivities, lies beside it.

The one-time kindergarten and elementary school at 3 Fürdő Street was built in 1874. A second storey was added in 1879 for the council hall. Its gained its present form in 1887.

Interior of the Pécs synagogue

The nursing home at the corner of Tímár and Goldmark Street was built in 1939 according to Antal Forbáth's plans. Today it is a state nursing home, where the elderly members of the Jewish community are also cared for.

The memorial plaque marking the site of the ghetto is set on the walls of the so-called MÁV (Hungarian Railway) House. The Jews of Pécs and from the surrounding area were taken to the railway station and herded into the cattle trains taking them to their death from this building.

The large, walled cemetery at Szív Street contains a number of magnificent grave memorials. The memorial to the victims of the Holocaust and a grave containing soap-bars made from the bodies of the Jews murdered in Auschwitz was erected near the large, renovated funeral parlour. The grave of the illustrious Jánosi-Engel family lies in this cemetery. The ennobled family played a prominent role in the economy and the political life of Pécs and Hungary.

Along the Danube

We take Road 11 from Budapest along the right bank of the Danube.

Szentendre

This picturesque small town lies about 20 km from Budapest. It is a popular tourist attraction owing to its many sights and monuments, and its narrow, winding streets suffused with a Mediterranean atmosphere. One of the many museums is a small Jewish museum, which on occasion also served as a synagogue. The museum was founded on a private initiative to preserve the memory of the Jewish community living in the town and the neighbouring area which perished in the Holocaust. (3 Alkotmány Street. Opening times: Tuesday–Sunday 11 a.m. to 5 p.m., closed from November 5 to March 15.)

Esztergom

According to the Jewish Lexicon of 1929, the oldest Jewish community of Hungary lived in this town. The first Jewish settlers arrived from Slavic and German territories well before the Hungarian Conquest period and they were joined by the Khazarian Jews, who arrived together with the Magyar tribes. Most historians assume that by 1050, the Jews had a community leadership, a prayer-house and a charitable fund for supporting the needy and the sick. The town had a separate Jewish quarter. The Jewish cemetery is first mentioned in a 1326 charter.

The community living in the town established at the intersection of major roads was first protected by the royal court and then by the chapter. By the early sixteenth century, the Jews numbered about eight hundred. After the Battle of Mohács in 1526 and the town's occupation by the Turkish army, most of the Jews living in Esztergom were rounded up and taken to Turkey. The remaining Jews preserved and maintained their institutions during the Ottoman period. The community was re-established during the earlier eighteenth century: a gravestone in the cemetery dates from 1775. The community created the institutions necessary for religious life. The already existing synagogue was rebuilt in 1858 and then enlarged again in 1888. This synagogue still stands today. The Jewish community was largest in 1914 (numbering about one thousand). After this, it diminished and perished almost completely during the Holocaust.

The former synagogue (today the House of Science in Galamb Street) by the foot of Tamás Hill was designed by Lipót Baumhorn. The main façade of the colourful, Moorish style building is divided into three parts. In the centre is the arcaded, open vestibule with a round window above it, flanked by two wings with pilasters onto which small onion domes have been set. The decorative cornice, the uniform windows and doors emphasize the building's harmony. An ornate tower tops the low dome.

The Auschwitz memorial, evoking human suffering in memory of the town's perished Jewish inhabitants, was erected in front of the synagogue.

For the next destinations, we take Road 51 on the left bank of the Danube.

Apostag

The best-known sight of this small town is the synagogue built in 1768 at 3 Iskola Street. The exterior of the Late Baroque building with a Classicist façade (a listed monument) has faithfully preserved the original form. The former synagogue now accom-

Kőszeg, Synagogue

Pécs, Interior of the Synagogue

modates a cultural centre, a library and a room dedicated to the memory of Lajos Nagy, a popular Hungarian writer. The original interior – the three, vaulted naves, the elaborate Ark, the *bimah*, the gallery and a part of the interior decoration – has also been carefully preserved. The exemplary renovation, designed by Péter Wirth, was awarded the Europa Nostra Prize.

A gravestone from 1650 has been found in the cemetery opposite the synagogue, proving that the Jewish community of Apostag had existed by that time.

Baja

The great synagogue at 9 Munkácsy Mihály Street is perhaps the most attractive Classicist building in Baja. The main adornment of the courtyard façade is the porch with its double row of columns and the tympanum crowning the colonnade. The synagogue was dedicated in 1845. The women's gallery on the two sides divides the interior into three naves. The central, high nave is covered with a handsomely painted, vaulted ceiling. The Ark is set in the centre of the *mizrah* (the eastern wall); above the Ark are the Tablets of the Law emerging from the cloud of smoke. The former Central Board of Hungarian Jews sold the building to the local council in the 1970s. In 1985, the local library was relocated to the renovated and transformed building. Careful interior architectural work has preserved the original atmosphere of the interior, while ensuring that the transformed building fulfils its new role. The ritual furnishings of the synagogue – the hand washbasin in the vestibule, the ornate charity box, the Ark and the *bimah* with its ornate railing – have been carefully restored.

The former Jewish school stood beside the synagogue. The monumental, arcaded memorial to the victims of the Holocaust was also erected beside the synagogue.

The Jewish cemetery lies on the road to Szeged.

Ede Telcs, the renowned Jewish sculptor, was born in Baja.

Jánoshalma

The first documentary evidence for the presence of Jews dates from 1782. Petőfi Street, where the synagogue lies, was formerly called Zsidótemplom [Jewish Temple] Street. Built in 1850, the synagogue is a rather small building in the Romantic style, which has recently been beautifully renovated and it is thus one of the few surviving rural synagogues preserving its original beauty. Its interior furnishings, however, have sadly been removed.

The Great Hungarian Plain

We leave Budapest on the M5 motorway for the first excursion.

Nagykőrös

The synagogue of this old community at 21 Rákóczi Street was built in 1925 according to the plans of Lajos Molnár. The main façade is divided into three parts and is crowned with a parapet and cornice; the building's other distinctive features are the roof ornaments, the ogee arch above the main entrance and two staircases decorated with stalactite motifs leading to the gallery. The interior of the synagogue is furnished in the traditional style. Beside the synagogue stands the office building of the community and the one-time Jewish school, whose street wall bears the memorial plaque of the ghetto. There is still a small, but active congregation loyal to Jewish traditions. The cemetery on the town's outskirts is well-tended.

Kecskemét

On the evidence of surviving charters and other documents, Jews had already lived in Kecskemét during the Ottoman period. The congregation was officially founded in 1744. One typical element of the townscape, the Great Synagogue at 2 Kaszap Street, was dedicated in 1781. This synagogue is one of the finest examples of Romantic architecture in Hungary. The arched triple entrance, flanked by two pilasters, the three small windows and the large ornate round window above them are the main adornments of the main façade, together with the decorative cornice and the central onion-domed tower. The synagogue's interior was rebuilt in the 1950s; a series of smaller roms were created and the building now functions as the House of Science.

Another interesting monument is the one-time Orthodox synagogue (12 Katona József Square). Built in 1913, the synagogue was renovated in the

Kőszeg, Synagogue

Mád, Synagogue

early 1990s and re-opened as the Museum of Photography. The building is a listed monument; its ceiling is covered with a lovely fresco, depicting the four symbolic animals and inscribed with a Hebrew text: "Be bold as a leopard, and swift as an eagle, and fleet as a hart, and strong as a lion" (Pirke Avot, V: 30).

The rebuilt office building and prayer house at 5 Nagykőrösi Street is used for community events and religious services by the small Jewish community still practicing its faith. The cemetery with its mortuary transformed into a memorial for the victims of the Holocaust lies along the road to Budapest.

Szolnok

The first Jewish families settled in Szolnok around 1830. At first they were only allowed to enter the town on market-days and in accordance with the regulation, they had to leave before nightfall. The congregation was officially founded in 1850 and births only began to be registered from 1851.

Although the first Jewish settlers were merchants, there soon emerged a layer of intellectuals, civil servants, lawyers, doctors and entrepreneurs. Most Jews settled in the area extending from the town centre to the Tisza river. They had two synagogues, schools and other institutions. There is still a small, active congregation.

The former great synagogue at 2 Templom Road in the park by the river has been transformed into an exhibition hall. The synagogue was built in 1898 by Lipót Baumhorn, the best-known synagogue architect. It was raised on a rectangular groundplan measuring 19.83 m by 34.19 m, with a main interior hall measuring 17.95 m by 17.85 m. Lipót Baumhorn drew many elements from his master, Ödön Lechner (the dome bears a striking resemblance to the dome of the Museum of Applied Arts in Budapest), although the design also shows the influence of Italian and German architecture. The building's distinctive features include the triple arch of the entrance, the emphatic central axis, the large round windows and the symmetrically placed arched double windows. The religious symbols and original furnishings were removed from the interior and thus only the beauty of the original architecture has survived. Inside the building, the dome rests on lavishly carved columns. The one-time women's gallery has also been left in its place.

Szeged

The letter-patent issued by King Charles III in Luxemburg on May 21, 1719 for the town of Szeged clearly states the following: "It is the duty of the town council to decide whether or not to admit and accept burghers and settlers; whether or not to tolerate Jews and Gypsies." The surviving documentary evidence indicates that Jews first settled in the town under Emperor Joseph II, between 1780–85. In 1808, the town had 375 Jewish inhabitants, one whole-sale merchant (Fülöp Wodianer), ten merchants, thirty-four peddlers, five artisans and one arendar (the *arenda* was a system of leasing property, such as landholdings, mills, inns, etc.).

The regulations of the Jewish community, modelled on the usual community by-laws *(takkanot)*, were drawn up in 1791. These regulations included a passage according to which it was the beadle's task to do a round of the community members and summon them to prayer by knocking on their door. In 1801, the community drew up new by-laws, according to which the rabbi and the beadle would be paid each week from the *gabella*, an internal communal tax collected by the community's administrators. The first synagogue was built in 1803. (At the same time, residence permits for the first settlers of the Calvinist faith were first issued in 1805.)

In 1813, a so-called settlement area was designated for the Jews between the two town quarters known as Palánk and Rókus in the southern part of Szeged. The Jews were first allowed to sell their wares in permanent shops in 1839. A year later they were also permitted to establish factories. In the later nineteenth century, the Jews of Szeged founded a number of factories for processing agricultural products: steam mills, distilleries, a vinegar factory, a match factory, tanneries, brickworks. They also established banks and various business firms. The first school was built in 1840. The Szeged community always placed great emphasis on the dissemination and use of the Hungarian language and national culture.

One interesting historical event occurred at Szeged: on July 28, 1849, after moving first to Debrecen and then to Szeged, the National Assembly enacted the Nationality Bill on the proposal of Prime Minister Bertalan Szemere, which declared the following: "Dismissing any differences in respect of rights and obligations as regards the citizens of the country professing differing faiths, it is hereby declared in accordance with this principle that inhabitants of the Mosaic faith who were born or have lawfully settled within the borders of the Hungarian State shall enjoy the same political and civic rights as the inhabitants of all other faiths."

Following the crushing of the War of Independence, Haynau imposed a huge collective fine on the Jews of Szeged and imprisoned the protesting delegates. One indication of the patriotism of the Szeged Jews was that on 10 December, 1850, they elected Lipót Löw to be their rabbi – the same Lipót Löw, who served as an army chaplain during the War of Independence and was imprisoned for three months in Pest. The rabbi demonstratively wore Hungarian clothes and his opinion was that "the synagogue should embrace the Hungarian language, and we hope that Hungary will embrace the synagogue." Lipót Löw's activity opened a magnificent chapter in the history of not only the Szeged community, but of Hungarian Jewry. He was an erudite, enlightened man, a greatly respected scholar. He was succeeded by his son, Immanuel Löw in 1878, who perished in the Holocaust. The Jews of Szeged played a prominent role in the town's economic and cultural life. Mór Kármán, the acclaimed educator, who reformed the national secondary school system, was a native of Szeged, as was Béla Balázs, writer and film critic, Ede Kisteleki, the poet, and Albert Wodianer, head of the well-known banker family, who was granted the title of baron in 1886 and elected to the Upper House of Hungarian Parliament.

In 1927, there were some eight thousand Jews in Szeged. Today, the greatly shrunken community still maintains its institutions and religious life.

Opening from the London Boulevard section of the Grand Boulevard in Szeged, Gutenberg Street leads to one of the town's most majestic monuments, the perhaps loveliest synagogue of Hungary.

The Great Synagogue at 14–16 Jósika Street was built in 1903 according to the plans of Lipót Baumhorn, the best known synagogue architect in Hungary. Of the twenty-four synagogues designed by Baumhorn, the one in Szeged is perhaps the most beautiful, a magnificent masterpiece of the Art Nouveau style in Szeged. An indication of the building's monumental dimensions is that the distance between the columns supporting the dome, i.e. the width of the nave is 20 m. The outer height of the dome is 48.5 m, its inner height is 32 m. The synagogue lies in the centre of a garden enclosed by an ornate iron fence. A flight of steps leads to the large, triple doorway, through which one enters the vestibule. A marble plaque in the vestibule lists the names of the victims of the Holocaust from Szeged. Two black coffins symbolize the most vulnerable victims: the children and the elderly. A plaque commemorating the Jews deported to the death camps from the re-annexed territory of Yugoslavia was dedicated in 1968.

The synagogue's harmony is enhanced by the white, blue and gold coloured ornamentation. The interior reflects Immanuel Löw's vision. The decoration of the cupola symbolizes the world: the twenty-four columns of the cupola drum represent the twenty-four hours of the day, the white flowers on a blue base of the burning bush symbolize faith, while the immenseness of the universe is denoted by the stars crafted from blue glass. The centre of the dome is set off by a Star of David around which the sun illuminates the sky. The elaborate painted decoration, the ingenious use of various colours and ornamental motifs, the Hebrew and Hungarian inscriptions, the floral patterns reflect both the Hungarianness and the Jewishness of the synagogue's builders.

The keystone of the pulpit's podium was made from Jerusalem marble; underneath it is a description of the synagogue's construction history. The doors of the Ark, decorated with lovely metal mounts, was carved from acacia, the Biblical *shittah* tree (the Ark was made by Ede Vogel). Eighteen Torah scrolls are kept in the nine compartments of the Ark. The rabbi holds the sermons from the pulpit above the *bimah*. The canopy above the Ark is a miniaturized version of the dome. The organ, made by Lipót Wegenstein in 1903, is set above the Ark. The double-manual instrument has twenty-four registers and 1276 pipes. The seven-branched menorahs were based on the descriptions in the Bible and the depictions on the Arch of Titus.

The interior ornamentation and the stained glass windows, reflecting the sequence of Jewish holy days, were made by Miksa Róth, again according to Immánuel Löw's vision. The five windows on the right depict daily work, the trumpet of Jericho, the purity and the iniquity of the soul, as well as the tents evoking the memory of the forty years' wandering in the wilderness, followed by scenes of rejoicing. The windows on the other side are decorated with depictions of the ritual artefacts used during the Shabbat, the Tablets of the Law, the burning bush, Rachel's grave mound, the Torah scrolls and the Wailing Wall. The large, many-branched chandeliers and the memorial plaques on the wall are also noteworthy. The elaborately carved benches were made by craftsmen from Szeged, as were the interior furnishing of the synagogue. The ironwork was made by Pál Fekete.

The synagogue can be visited during specific opening times (Monday–Friday and Sunday: 10 a.m. to 12. a.m. and 13 p.m. to 17 p.m., closed Saturdays and on Jewish holidays; a guide can be requested from the community office at 20 Gutenberg Street).

The old synagogue lies at 12 Hajnóczy Street (parallel to Gutenberg Street). The Jews settling in Szeged requested permission from the council to purchase a plot of land and to build temple in 1789; the first synagogue was eventually built in 1803. This simple building proved too small and a new synagogue was built in its place in 1843. The synagogue designed by Henrik and József Lipovszky measured 16.5 m by 29.9 m, the cornice height is 10.4 m, and its interior covers 344 m^2. The synagogue could seat 400 men and 260 women. This building is one of the most outstanding pieces of Neo-Classicist architecture in Szeged. Its fine construction materials, the Tuscan order, the harmonious proportions are most remarkable. The three-nave interior too corresponds to the Classicist ideal. A plaque inscribed in Hebrew and Hungarian shows the level of the flood on March 12, 1879. The white marble slab on the synagogue's wall commemorates the soldiers fallen during the Great War.

The vestibule has a beautiful washbasin of red marble; the walls are covered with plaques bearing the names of the victims of the Holocaust. Set against the eastern wall, the Ark is crowned by a tympanum and flanked by simple, elegant columns and arches. The Tablets of the Law above the Ark are decorated with lion motifs. The women's gallery encloses the interior in a U shape. The furnishings of the synagogue have been removed – the building is in the possession of the local council. The one-time Jewish school is located beside the synagogue.

The community office building at 20 Gutenberg Street were designed by Lipót Baumhorn in the same style as the great synagogue. Completed in 1903, the building accommodates the offices of the Szeged community and of the neigbouring area, the winter prayer room, the council hall, and a kosher kitchen and dining hall (kosher meals can be obtained by prior arrangement). The rabbi's flat and the nursing home for the elderly are also housed here.

The large, ornate council hall bears witness to the former prosperity of the Jewish community. The dynamic, elaborate architecture of the vaulted hall decorated with white, blue and gold painting has large-size portraits of the one-time religious and secular leaders of the community on its walls. The hall is lit by a huge, flamboyant chandelier. Major holidays, cultural events and community meetings are held in this hall. Though strongly decimated, the Jewish community of Szeged continues to maintain a lively and intensive community and cultural life.

The Jewish quarter lay around the synagogues and the office building. Most of the streets and their houses have an interesting story to tell. Between 1880 and 1911, Bólyai János Street was called Zsinagóga [Synagogue] Street, while Jósika Street was called Löw Lipót Street between 1912 and 1941. A memorial plaque on the wall of the house at 8 Hajnóczy Street records that Chief Rabbi Immánuel Löw lived in the vicinity of the old synagogue. The text of the plaque mentions that Löw wrote one of his main studies, *Die Flora der Juden* while under house arrest between April 23, 1920 and June 11, 1921, under the counter-revolutionary regime. Mikszáth Kálmán Street used to be the commercial centre – there are still many small shops here. The first paprika and salami factory of the famous Pick family was located in present-day Gutenberg Street.

The large, walled Jewish cemetery lies on the road to Dorozsma (13 Fonógyári Road), next to the municipal cemetery. The attractive, spacious funeral parlour and the magnificent grave memorials evoke the memory of this once prosperous community.

Makó

In 2002, the local council renovated the Orthodox synagogue at 15 Eötvös Street with support from the Alliance of the Jewish Congregations of Hungary and the American Jewish community. Built in 1870, the small synagogue was designed in the decorative, Romantic style. The large Neolog synagogue, one of Lipót Baumhorn's masterpieces, was sold by the former Central Board of Hungarian Jews in 1946, and the building was subsequently demolished.

Northern and eastern Hungary

Taking Road 4 from Budapest, we can visit Debrecen, Nyíregyháza and Miskolc, from where the Pilgrim Route also starts.

Debrecen

The first Jewish families, who settled in the one-time free royal town in 1840, arrived from Hajdúsámson. By 1846, the Jewish community had its own walled burial ground. Quite a number of the Jewish soldiers in *honvéd* army of 1848–49 War of Independence came from the Debrecen community. The congregation was officially founded in 1852. The first synagogue was built in 1875, the first school in 1888. A new synagogue, a school, community offices, a ritual bath, a matzoh factory was built by the turn of the century, followed by a girls' school and an Orthodox synagogue in Kápolnás Street in 1909. The first provincial Jewish gymnasium was established in 1921, with Albert Kardos, a well-known literary scholar and historian, appointed as its headmaster. Under Chief Rabbi Sámuel Schlesinger's spiritual guidance, the Debrecen community became one of the most influential Status Quo congregations in Hungary. The town also had an Orthodox and a smaller Hassidic community.

The largest provincial community lives in Debrecen; it also acts as the centre for the smaller communities in the region and the "scattered remnants". The annual meeting of the representatives of the Hungarian-speaking Jewish communities from outside Hungary and the leaders and representatives of the Hungarian Jewish community takes place in Debrecen – this event has become an important event in the life of the Jewish communities in the Carpathian Basin.

The synagogue (the synagogue of the former school) and the office building lie next to each other. The pleasing proportions of the complex, built in the Eclectic style in 1909, can be seen from afar. (The magnificent great synagogue was demolished after the war.) The façade is dominated by the triple window and entrance. The synagogue's interior, ornamentation and furnishings have been superbly renovated. The office building accommodates the ceremonial hall, the club, the Talmud-Torah class and an excellent kosher restaurant. The community also maintains a kosher butchery and bakery.

The former Orthodox synagogue, built in 1913 in the Eclectic style (currently under renovation), the Orthodox prayer-house and the ritual bath *(mikveh)* are near the synagogue, at 6 Pásti Street.

Visitors can reserve accommodation at a discount by prior arrangement in the guesthouse by the synagogue (Panzió Bajcsy, Debrecen, 20 Bajcsy-Zsilinszky Street, +36 52 447 146), and arrangements can also be made to visit the kosher winery at Erdőbénye (Erdőbénye, 1 Kossuth Street, + 36 47 396 102, illespince@illespince.hu).

The cemetery can be found on Monostorpályi Road.

The Pilgrim Route

The Pilgrim Route takes us to the one-time heartland of Hungarian Hassidism and the graves of the Hassidic rabbis of Hungary, evoking the still vivid legends and traditions associated with them. In addition to the colourful and unique ethnographic and religious traditions awaiting discovery, the route itself leads through a beautiful part of Hungary. With its historic towns and picturesque villages, the entire region offers an unforgettable experience.

The Pilgrim Route can be reached in several ways from Budapest: the shortest leads through Miskolc by taking the M3 Motorway from Budapest and then Road 37 to Sátoraljaújhely. The other recommended route starts from Debrecen with a detour to Nagykálló, and then continuing on Road 38 and Road 37 to Sátoraljaújhely.

Prior to World War 1, northern and northeastern Hungary – the Zemplén region, the Bodrogköz area and the Upper Tisza region – was populated by large Orthodox Hassidic communities. These deeply religious Jews, with their distinctive costume of kaftans and fur hats, their earlocks and long beards, made their living from trade in wine and agricultural produce, or as vintners and carters, or artisans. In the centre of Hassidic life stood the rabbi (whom they called their *rebbe* or *tzaddik*, the miracle-working rabbi), to whom his followers flocked by the thousands to seek solace and advice for their spiritual and other problems. In their eyes, the *rebbe* was, by virtue of his piety, the best qualified to intercede with God on mankind's behalf. The *rebbe* also acted as a judge in the everyday disputes of his followers. (*Tzaddik* means "righteous".) Their graves still attract many pilgrims, who write their requests onto small slips of paper (called *kvittel*) and then place them into the cracks of the burial monuments, convinced that their requests will be fulfilled.

This colourful, interesting community perished almost completely during the Holocaust; their memory is now preserved by a few village cemeteries. The graves of the famed rabbis are usually set in the most prominent section of these cemeteries.

The Pilgrim Route takes us through picturesque, rural areas left mostly untouched by modern industry, and through lovely villages, which once had important Jewish communities. However, not one single active congregation exists in these villages.

We begin the journey by taking Road 4 from Debrecen to Nagykálló.

Nagykálló

One of the most interesting stops on the Pilgrim Route is the former seat of Szabolcs county. Although the exact date when the Jewish community was established remains uncertain, the first settlers apparently arrived several hundred years ago, The town was destroyed three times and although the Jews moved elsewhere after each catastrophe, they always returned. We know that there was an organised community in the town by the mid-eighteenth century.

Isaac Taub (or Reb Eizik Taub in Yiddish), the founder of Hungarian Hassidism, the perhaps best known Hungarian *tzaddik*, was elected rabbi in 1781. He was a remarkable man, who lived a most unusual life. His ancestors had fled the Spanish Inquisition in the seventeenth century and settled in Szerencs. He studied under Rabbi Shmuel Shmelke Horowitz of Nikolsburg in Bohemia, then returned to Hungary and became a teacher in Nagykálló. He lived among herdsmen and shepherds in the field, where he grew to love nature. His only source of amusement were the Bible and the shepherds' pipe. The song of the Kalever Rebbe was born in these fields.

The rooster is crowing,
The dawn is coming,
In the green field, in the flat field,
A bird promenades.

What a bird,
What a bird!
With its blue leg, with its green wings
It waits for me and sings.

Wait, bird, wait,
You must always wait,
If God chose you to be my mate
I will be yours.

According to the Hassidic legend, he learnt the song from a shepherd, who sold it to him and then immediately forgot it. The Kalever Rebbe added a verse in Hebrew to the original song.

When shall it be,
Oh when shall it be?
Yiboneh hamikdosh, ir Tziojn temallei
(May the Temple be rebuilt, the City of Zion replenished),
Then shall it be!
Why is it not now,
Oh why is it not now?
Umipnei hatoeinu golinu meartzeinu,
(For our sins we have been driven from our country),
That's why it is not now!"

His followers soon learnt the song and expressed their sorrow and their yearning for the Messianic Age with this song, thinking that if their rabbi sang it, they could hardly be faulted for doing the same. There was no Jewish wedding or festivity in the region, where this song was not sung.

The rabbi's fame spread swiftly, and people flocked to him by the thousands. There were several legends about him already during his lifetime, and his unusual life inspired many writers and poets. His followers still form a vibrant community in the US and in Israel (Bne Brak), where one of his descendants proudly styles himself as the Kalever Rebbe. Only a few families remain of the original community, which once numbered over one thousand. Their synagogues and other institutions have disappeared or have been transformed. Their memory is now preserved by the legends and two cemeteries.

Eizik Taub's grave, set in an *ohel* (a tent shaped structure built over the tomb) lies in the old, walled cemetery on Nagybalkányi Road (near the railway station), which still preserves its original form. Built of red and yellow bricks. the *ohel* is a small building in the traditional style. The inscription of the simple gravestone was written by the *rebbe*: "Here lies Rebbe Eizik, rabbi of the holy community of Nagy-kálló. An upright Jew. He died at 70 years of age, on the 7th of Adar in 5589 (i.e. 1829)." Many come to visit his grave on his *yahrzeit*. (Caretaker: Gábor Braun, tel.: +36 30 248 6379.)

The new cemetery on Akácos Street, ringed by a wall of concrete, too has two burials of importance. One is the grave of Rabbi Emánuel (Menachem) Bródy, who maintained a famous *yeshiva* in the early twentieth century. His *ohel* is surrounded by several hundred graves. The painter Imre Ámos, sometimes called the Hungarian Chagall, was born in Nagykálló and many of his painting were based on local legends from this area. He perished in the Holocaust.

Leaving Nagykálló, we continue to Nyírbátor through Kállósemjén.

Nyírbátor

The congregation was founded by Simon Mendel and his five sons. The Mendel family continued to play an important role in the community's life. None of the town's former 160 Jewish inhabitants live here, the community's memory is preserved by the cemetery.

We take Road 471 to Mátészalka.

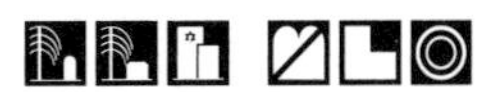

Mátészalka

The first Jewish families arrived to the seat of one-time royal county of Szatmár in the mid-eighteenth century. Parallel to the growth of the community, the necessary institutions were established. The first synagogue was erected in 1828. The town had a Sephardic prayer house, a school, several rabbi's houses, a *mikveh,* and other institutions. The ranks of renowned persons born in Mátészalka include Dr. Gyula Szalkai, who introduced public lighting in his home town (the first rural town in Hungary to boast this amenity), and Tony Curtis, the American movie star, as well as Ignác Strasnoff, the infamous confidence trickster, who "sold" Váci Street in Budapest. The town had about 1600 Jewish inhabitants before the war, of whom only a few families remain today.

Built in 1857, the synagogue is aligned perpendicular to the street on a fairly large, longish plot at 37 Kossuth Lajos Street. The stone frame of the entrance is inscribed with a verse from the Psalms and the construction date. There is a tympanum above the entrance. The main façade is pierced by three arched windows, above which rises a tripartite attic, decorated with a Star of David in its centre, and a Hebrew inscription above it: "Make me a sanctuary, that I may dwell among them" (Exodus, 2: 25: 8). The wall facing the courtyard has arched windows. The staircase leading to the women's gallery was built on this side.

The U shaped gallery, provided with a plain railing, is supported by six pillars with finely carved heads. The plaques commemorating the victims of the Holocaust are set on the two sides of the entrance. The simple *bimah*, the platform for the desk from which the Torah is read, is set in the centre. Above the unpretentiously ornamented Ark is a round window. The synagogue has a handsomely painted ceiling. Its interior furnishings are rather plain.

There were several buildings behind the synagogue in the longish courtyard: the council hall, the former rabbi's house, the cantor's house and the butchery. The synagogue is in a rather bad state of preservation, the other buildings have collapsed by now – only the rabbi's house is in a more or less acceptable condition.

Similarly to most rural towns, the Jews of Mátészalka settled in one neighbourhood: the relics of Jewish life all lie in Kossuth, Rákóczi and Zöldfa Streets. The ritual bath was in Rákóczi Street, opening from Kossuth Lajos Street; the building was transformed into a synagogue after the war, and later sold. It is currently a residential building. The one-time Jewish school and kindergarten can be seen at 19–21 Rákóczi Street. Strolling further, the next sight is the house of the Hassidic rabbi, and turning into Zöldfa Street, we find the building of the former Sephardic synagogue *(bet hamidrash)*, now also converted into a residential building.

One of the striking features of the two hundred years old, walled, well-tended cemetery in Felleg-vár Street is the wooden *ohel* facing the entrance (a rather uncommon feature since most were constructed from stone or bricks). Rabbi Haim Fajs lies buried here. To the right are two finely carved gravestones, marking the burial of Menasse Grünbaum and his wife. The cemetery contains a number of lovely old gravestones. The oldest ones, often several hundred years old, are on the right side. A few gravestones in the centre are covered with a metal case to protect them from rain and snow. (The caretaker lives in the house next to the cemetery.)

Road 41 takes us to Nyíregyháza.

Nyíregyháza

The first Jewish families settled in the town during the later nineteenth century. The town prospered and grew rapidly, indicated also by the fact that in 1875, the seat of Szabolcs county was transferred from Nagykálló to Nyíregyháza. The growing number of Jewish inhabitants too played a vital role in the development of the town's industry and trade. Nyíregyháza had a thriving Jewish population until the Holocaust. The community was about five thousand strong, it had several synagogues, schools, butcheries and other institutions. Today there is a relatively small, active community, which maintains its religious and community life together with the necessary institutions.

Built between 1924 and 1932, the imposing synagogue at 6 Mártírok Square was designed by Lipót Baumhorn. Its plain, puritanical walls and large windows, the elegant ornamentation make it one of the town's main attractions. The apsidal niche for the Ark protrudes from the eastern façade facing Síp Street. The two staircases, flanked by pilasters, leading to the gallery were built on two sides of the original entrance. The currently used entrance is set into the long wall facing the courtyard. The well-designed main entranceway with a large, decorative window above it, is on the western side.

The *bimah* is set in the centre of the spacious synagogue. The eastern wall, the *mizrah*, is lavishly decorated. The Ark is flanked by double Corinthian columns connected by an arch with lacework decoration, and an ornate round window has been set above it. The wall-painting above the Ark depicts two huge, rearing lions holding a ribbon inscribed with a Hebrew quote from the Psalms.

Women were originally relegated to the U shaped gallery; today, one row of benches has been set aside for them.

The winter prayer-house, the culture hall, the offices, a guest room and a small museum can be found in the newly renovated office building beside the synagogue.

The walled, well-tended cemetery, made up of two parts, lies on Kótaji Road (beside Road 4 leading to Debrecen). One part of the burial ground established around 1840 was used by the Status Quo congregation, the other by the Orthodox one. A large memorial to the victims of the Holocaust, inscribed with the names of the perished Jews of Nyíregyháza, was erected in its central section. (The caretaker's house is in the cemetery; tel.: +36 42 473 290.)

From Nyíregyháza we take Road 4 to Kisvárda.

Kisvárda

The first Jewish families settled in the town, lying at the intersection of major roads, in the later eighteenth century with the help of the Esterházy family. The congregation was formed in 1796 and soon afterwards, in 1801, a synagogue was erected. Abraham Jichak Weinberger was one of the community's famous rabbis.

In 1941, the Jewish community numbered 3770; they had several synagogues, prayer houses, a *mikveh*, a butchery and other institutions. Today, there is no congregation in the town.

The large, superbly renovated synagogue in Dimitrov Street (formerly called Csillag Street) is currently an exhibition hall. Its exterior preserves the original form, while the interior has been redesigned in accordance with the building's new function. Built in 1901 in the Romanticising style, the red brick building's appeal is greatly enhanced by the white stone windows and entrances, the decorative pilasters and the façade ornaments, as well as the large stained glass windows of varied form and the domed metal roofing. The plaque commemorating the victims of the Holocaust is set on the building.

The former winter prayer room lay in the grey building by the synagogue's western wall. Its interior furnishing are traditional, with a few articles brought over from the synagogue.

The burial of the local, renowned rabbi lies in the cemetery.

A small detour towards Záhony, the border, takes us to the next destination.

Mándok

The cemetery of the settlement near the Ukrainian border preserves the memory of the former flourishing Jewish community.

From Mándok we return to Nyíregyháza and take Road 38 to Tokaj.

Tokaj

The first Jewish wine merchants settled in this picturesque town in the seventeenth century. There is documentary evidence that they had founded a burial society by 1750. The wealthy Jewish merchants lived in the magnificent, spacious merchant houses on Fő Street. (Some of these houses are still called "Jewish houses" by the locals.) The synagogue and the other community buildings lay around the Kispiac [Small Market] and Alsó Street. The community's most famed rabbi was Dávid Schück, who was active from 1846 until his death in 1899. The town had a sizeable Jewish community of around a thousand before World War 2, of which only a few families can be found today.

The area around Alsó Street was the focus of the one-time Jewish community: the synagogue, the school, the community buildings, the butchery, the bakery and the ritual bath were all located here.

The rabbi, the community's spiritual leader, and the employees of the community too lived here. The great synagogue, one of the town's sights, lies in this area.

The domed building of the synagogue, with its round gable windows, is a prominent feature of the townscape. This spacious, harmoniously proportioned building with its ornate portico in the Romantic (Moorish) style was built in 1890 in place of the small, eighteenth century synagogue, which had been destroyed by fire the same year. The main façade of the magnificent, harmonious building is dominated by the arched central pilasters and the ornate portico. The synagogue survived World War 2, when German troops used it as a stable, but during the decades after the war, its condition deteriorated because the remnants of the Jewish community were unable to raise the funds for the necessary renovations. The former Central Board of Hungarian Jews eventually sold the building and its roof was dismantled. In the late 1980s, the National Monuments Board, the local council and other organizations joined efforts to save the building on a local initiative. The roofing was repaired first, in order to protect the synagogue from further deterioration. Unfortunately, children built a fire in the unguarded building – the roof burnt down and had to be rebuilt again. The building is now roofed with a lovely copper dome. The building will be used for cultural purposes and there are plans for creating a Holocaust memorial room on the upper storey (in what will be the domed hall). The names of the victims of the Holocaust from Tokaj-Hegyalja and the Zemplén region will be inscribed on sixty-seven plaques.

Other plans include the creation of a cultural centre and a park around the synagogue, currently one of the most neglected areas in the historic town centre. This will include the renovation of the one-time Jewish community office building (currently functioning as a tenement block), and the building's transformation into a cultural centre, as well as a Jewish education, tourist and pilgrimage centre. In order to achieve this, the local council and the recently founded Tokaj-Hegyalja Jewish Cultural Heritage Association have pooled their efforts.

The single still active synagogue in the Tokaj-Hegyalja region can be found beside the former great synagogue. The small, finely renovated building, a former *bet hamidrash,* is ornamented with a Star of David. It was originally the prayer-house of the Hassidim before the war.

The old cemetery can be reached by taking the ferry. The "old" cemetery founded in 1750 lies by the ruins of Tokaj Castle in the Bodrogzug. Since it lies on the floodplain and was repeatedly flooded, at the close of the nineteenth century the Jews were permitted to establish a burial ground in a higher-lying area, which they used from that time on. The picturesque old cemetery contains about fifteen old gravestones from the eighteenth and nineteenth century.

The new cemetery lies on Bodrogkeresztúri Road, on the outskirts of the town. This burial ground was established at the turn of the century. The large, well-tended, walled burial ground on the slope of Kopaszhegy (Mt. Kopasz) overlooks the river. The cemetery contains some three hundred burials, with the oldest gravestones – brought here from the old cemetery – dating from the nineteenth century. The best-known rabbis buried here are Dávid Schück and Akiba Strasser. There are only burial mounds in front of the *ohel* containing the gravestones; the *kvittel* are set into the cracks of the gravestones. The other two graves were brought here from the old cemetery – according to the locals, one of them marked the burial of a rabbi called Fanféder, while the other remains enigmatic. (Contact person: Lajos Lőwy, 41 Rákóczi Road; tel.: +36 47 352 737, +36 47 353 730 or +36 30 327 1161.)

We continue our journey on Road 38.

Bodrogkeresztúr

The first Jews arrived to the small town on the banks of the Bodrog River in 1726. The small community prospered and grew stronger. One of the most important Hassidic communities emerged in this settlement. This Hassidic community grew stronger under the leadership of Jesája Steiner (1851–1925), the renowned *tzaddik* known as Reb Sájele. He studied under Rabbi Friedländer of Olaszliszka, moving to Bodrogkeresztúr after his death. Reb Sájele's fame grew and he was regarded as the successor of the Olaszliszka *tzaddik*. Jews and Gentiles alike came from afar to seek his advice. Many legends are told about him. It was said that he never slept, never rested, dozing in his armchair for many nights, meditating and praying.

There was a Gentile, who had lived separate from his wife for many years. One day, he visited the rabbi to ask his advice. The rabbi told him to wait, for he felt that his wife would come that very day. "Foolish Jew," thought the man, "I have not seen my wife for many years, why should we meet on this day?" That afternoon, however, the man's wife came to rabbi. She had regretted her decision never to speak to her husband again. The rabbi told his *shammes* to find the man, and then made the couple promise that they would make up. This couple went to the rabbi's burial, when he died.

It is said, that when Reb Sájele died, a fire broke out in the synagogue and consumed the table, where he used to pray, but his books were spared.

According to another story, lightning struck a house and it caught fire. The rabbi struck a knife into the beam, and the fire miraculously went out.

Reb Sájele's grave is still visited, especially on his *yahrzeit*, on the 3rd of Iyar.

The well-tended cemetery enclosed with a wall of stone slabs in the shape of stone tablets lies on the mountain covered with vineyards. Surrounded by the burials of his followers, Reb Sájele's grave is located on the highest point. The traditional *ohel* is provided with an iron door and contains three graves with finely carved, painted gravestones. The middle one marks the grave of Reb Sájele, one marks the burial of his wife, and the third of a rabbi whose name is not remembered by the locals. An opening for the *kvittel* can be found together with the remains of the memorial lights.

Reb Sájele Steiner

Stepping out from the *ohel*, the Zemplén landscape with its gently rolling hills, vineyards, small villages, unfolds before the visitor. There are many lovely old and new gravestones in the cemetery. (Caretaker: Mrs József Kádár, 9 Dózsa köz, tel.: +36 47 396 514.)

The former synagogue is at 57 Kossuth Street. The community had several other buildings in the town in addition to the former Neolog great synagogue. The large, yellow building is set back from the street; it was built on a small hillock overlooking the Bodrog River. The synagogue differs from the other plain houses beside it in that it has five pairs of large, trefoil arched windows and a gambrel roof. There is a good view of the meandering river from beside the lovely wrought iron fence in front of the façade facing the river.

The former rabbinical residence, Reb Sájele Steiner's house at 65 Kossuth Lajos Street has survived in an unaltered form. The windows of the renovated building with a four column porch open onto the street. The house is an excellent example of one-time rural architecture. Today it is a memorial house and a resting place for pilgrims. (Caretaker: László Bozsó, tel.: +36 47 396 030.)

Olaszliszka

This sleepy little town was the vibrant centre of Hungarian Hassidism in the late nineteenth century. Rabbi Hershele Friedman (1808–1874) attracted a huge following. His grave, set inside the carefully preserved *ohel* on the highest point of the picturesque cemetery on the hillside overlooking the Bodrog River, attracts countless pilgrims. The high wall of the cemetery and the parking lot behind the gate decorated with a menorah, renovated by generous funding from his American followers, can be seen from afar. Entering the cemetery, a path leads to the highest point of the hill, offering a lovely view of the cemetery filled with ancient gravestones. The rebbe's grave stands beside the entrance, as if guarding and protecting his followers. The finely preserved *ohel* contains three burials: Rabbi Friedman's in the centre, his wife, and their son-in-law, Rabbi Haim Friedländer, who was the master of Reb Sájele Steiner, mentioned above.

The opening for the *kvittel* is set into the copper plates covering the wooden frame of the grave, in front of the finely carved gravestones, surrounded by the candles left by the pilgrims. Many pilgrims visit the rabbi's grave on his *yahrzeit* on the 14th of Adar. There are about four hundred burials in the cemetery, some several hundred years old. The last gravestone was erected in 1978. The simple, worn stones, bearing traditional symbols, preserve the memory of the one-time community.

The ruins of the synagogue can be found on an abandoned plot overgrown with weeds (15 Kossuth Lajos Street). The large synagogue was probably built in the later nineteenth century. Only the eastern wall has survived with the niche for the Ark and traces of painting. Since no Jews were left in the town, the locals re-used the synagogue's stones and took away its furnishings. Film director Miklós Jancsó shot his three-part *Jelenlét* ("Presence") here and in the Jewish cemetery of Bodrogkeresztúr.

The cemetery can be found at 31 Belsőkocsord Street. (Caretaker: Mrs Ödön Krajnyák, Belsőkocsord Street 25, tel.: +36 47 58 042).

Erdőbénye

One of the wine-growing communities of the Hegyalja region, which used to be in part inhabited by Jews engaged in wine-making and the wine trade. There used to be a kosher guesthouse in this popular holiday resort. Today, only the cemetery preserves the memory of the one-time Jewish community. There is a kosher winery in the village.

We continue towards Tolcsva.

Tolcsva

One of the best-known wine-growing villages of the Hegyalja region lies on the Bodrog River. The Jewish inhabitants were engaged in wine production and the wine trade. The Jewish community's memory is preserved by the cemetery.

We return to Road 37 to continue our journey.

Sátoraljaújhely

The origins of the Jewish community can be traced to the eighteenth century. The first documentary evidence comes from 1771, when the congregation was formed. Between 1808 and 1840, the famed Moses Teitelbaum, one of the founders of Hungarian Hassidism – known also as Yismach Moshe after his main work – was the community's rabbi. He was born in Przemysl in 1759. (The name Teitelbaum comes from German *Dattelbaum,* meaning fig-tree.) He was the scion of a renowned family of rabbinic scholars. He was chosen rabbi of Sátoraljaújhely in 1808, where he founded a famous *yeshiva* in which he taught for thirty-three years. He was known far and wide for his erudition and ascetism, and he was visited by countless Hassidic pilgrims. His followers called him "Old Saint". His fame spread among the Gentiles too and according to local lore, Lajos Kossuth, one of the later leaders of the 1848–49 War of Independence, had also visited him.

According to one version of this legend, Kossuth was brought before the rabbi by his mother when he was sick as a child; the rabbi healed him and blessed him with a Biblical verse. According to another version, Kossuth visited the rabbi during the years he was attending the gymnasium in the town. "A young lad from Monok, who was studying in the gymnasium of Újhely, once visited the rabbi. He took off his hat. The rabbi went up to him and placed his hand on the lad's head, and said: 'You shall be as the one who saw the burning bush. Your words shall ring far and wide, the Lord of the Hosts shall make your great, and grant you long life by the rivers of Babylon'."

The rabbi always kept his cane and his festive clothes by his bed, so that if the Messiah came, he would be able to receive him without delay. Friday afternoons the rabbi would climb Mt. Sátor, from where one could see afar, for he believed that the Messiah would arrive right before the Shabbat. Then he would return disappointedly to the synagogue, in the hope that the miracle would come to pass the next week. After his death, a poor lad was hired, whose task it was to climb atop Mt. Sátor on Friday afternoon to await the Messiah.

Rabbi Teitelbaum's followers flocked to their master's grave after his death. The trains were filled with pilgrims on the day of his *yahrzeit* – in the 1920s even the Hungarian-Czechoslovak border was opened, and pilgrims were allowed to cross into Hungary even if they lacked the necessary travel documents. Visitors continue to visit his grave, especially on his *yahrzeit* on the 28th of Tammuz.

The community flourished between the 1880s and the outbreak of World War 1. After 1886, the community split into three: there was a Status Quo congregation, an Orthodox one and a Hassidic one, the latter having seceded from the Orthodox. Each congregation had its own synagogue, prayer-house, school and other institutions. Called the Kaesztenbaum School after its benefactor, the school founded by the Status Quo congregation functioned for over one hundred years. This congregation also maintained a Jewish hospital. The sculptor József Engel and Mór Mezei, the famed Jewish politician active at the turn of the century, were both born here. Sátoraljaújhely had about four thousand Jewish inhabitants before the war, of whom only a few remain today. Two cemeteries and a small prayer house are all that survive of their institutions.

One of the destinations of the Pilgrim Route, the old cemetery lies along Road 37, opposite the Tobacco Factory. The several hundred years old cemetery on the hillside, enclosed by a modern concrete wall, can be seen from afar. The gate is ornamented with a menorah and leads to a small, open pavilion covered with a decorative copper dome.

This open structure functions as a waiting room, with stone benches set in a circle and a hand-washing basin in the centre. (According to the prescriptions of Judaism, one must wash one's hands in the traditional manner by repeatedly pouring water over them after leaving the cemetery.) A few steps lead to the *ohel* containing Moses Teitelbaum's grave.

The recently constructed modern, decorative building of unhewn stones, concrete and glass with its metal-mounted, dark brown wooden doors contains three graves. Two of them contain the burial of Moshe Teitelbaum and his wife, the third the burial of Alexander, the one-time rabbi of Komárom. Finely carved, painted gravestones mark the burials. In addition to being decorative, the painting also serves practical purposes: to make the worn Hebrew inscription legible. The burial is covered by a wooden chest provided with a copper lid with an opening, into which the pilgrims can place their *kvittel*. Candle holders and plaques inscribed with the prayers to be recited have been set on the walls of the *ohel*. Three stone slabs with a Hebrew inscription, dating from various periods, have been built into the wall, together with two grated windows with stone frames, protected by iron shutters, salvaged from old, demolished buildings. Small pathways lead to areas provided with benches under the windows. According to tradition, the Kohanites (descendants of the High Priest Aron) are not allowed to enter grave buildings and they usually recite the prayers outside, under an open window.

Beside the *ohel* is a lovely rabbi's grave under a small tree, enclosed by a wrought iron fence. The more or less identical, worn, broken, white gravestones are aligned into regular rows in the cemetery. These gravestones underwent many hardships during the centuries: they had been taken to the new cemetery and were then brought back. (The last burial in this cemetery took place about a hundred years ago.)

On the *yahrzeit* of the *rebbe* – on the 28th of Tammuz according to the Jewish calendar – the cemetery evokes the past. Large groups of pilgrims dressed in the traditional Orthodox Jewish garb visit the grave. The new, modern building of the ritual bath is located beside the cemetery. The pilgrims visiting the cemetery can comply with the prescription of ritual cleanliness. A resting place has also been created in the building. (Caretaker: Elek Varga, tel.: +36 30 995 8562.)

The other Jewish burial ground, known as the new cemetery, can be found in Kazinczy Street.

We start back on Road 37, and then take the road to Tarcal; turning left, we reach our next destination.

Tarcal

Although Jews had lived in Tarcal since the eighteenth century, the congregation was officially formed in the mid-nineteenth century. There was a synagogue, a school, and a nursing home. The congregation's best-known rabbi was Ezékiel Paneth, active between 1813–1822, who later became Chief Rabbi of Transylvania. The village had some three hundred Jewish inhabitants before the war, of whom none remain today. The small, Baroque synagogue is in a very bad state of preservation. The outer, covered stairway leading to the women's gallery was built against the rear end, with an arched gable above it. The arch of the stone framed entrance is decorated with floral motifs and a Hebrew inscription: "This gate of the Lord, into which the righteous shall enter!" (Psalm 118: 20). The *bimah* is set in the centre. Remains of the traditional, painted lion motifs survive on the eastern wall. The podium of the Ark is raised. The synagogue has an attractively painted ceiling. The gallery on the western side has a lovely wrought iron railing.

After returning to Road 37, we turn right towards Mád.

Mád

The first Jewish families settled in the wine-growing village of the Hegyalja region in 1726. By 1771, the community had a synagogue and a rabbi. Later still, an elementary school and a famed *yeshiva* were also maintained. The entire community perished in the Holocaust. The village appears in a Hungarian saying: "He's no nearer than the Jew from Mád!" According to the legend, a Jewish merchant from Mád set out on business on his cart, but fell asleep on the seat. His horse turned around and when he awoke, he found himself in front of his own house.

The recently renovated Baroque (Zopf) synagogue built in 1795 is unique among the Hungarian architectural relics from this period. It lies in the street parallel to the main street. The entrance to the finely renovated building, built on an oblong plan, is on the southern side. The attic of the eastern and western façade rises above the synagogue. The building is a testimony to the dynamism of contemporary Baroque architecture. Vase ornamentation in the Zopf style ornament the centre and the two sides of the façade. Three large, arched windows pierce the eastern wall; the staircase leading to the gallery was built against the western side. Passing through entrance with its the elaborately carved stone frame, the visitor walks through the vaulted vestibule before descending a few steps to enter the synagogue. The harmonious interior with its magnificent ornamentation reflects the excellent taste of the builders. The central bay of the nine-bay vaulting is supported by four pillars. The platform of the *bimah,* enclosed by a lovely wrought iron railing, is set between these pillars. Steps with an elaborately carved railing lead to the magnificent Ark set in the centre of the eastern wall. An intricate painted decoration covers the ceiling and the walls. The women's gallery with its openwork railing is set above the entrance and rests on two pillars.

The one-time rabbi's house and the *yeshiva* were erected opposite the synagogue. Both are masterpieces of rural Baroque architecture. The most magnificent view of this two-storey, arcaded building, an outstanding monument of the village, is from the Catholic church. The size of the building was necessitated by the great number of students studying in the *yeshiva.*

The Jewish cemetery lies on the edge of the village, on the hillside, and contains many lovely old gravestones.

From Mád, we continue our journey to Tállya.

Tállya

There were three synagogues in the settlement; the latest one was built in 1890. Most buildings of the one-time Jewish community were demolished or transformed. The walled, well-tended cemetery contains the burial of the grandson of Moses Teitelbaum, the renowned rabbi of Sátoraljaújhely. The memorial erected in 1974 preserves the memory of the 150 local Jews who perished in the Holocaust.

Leaving Tállya, we continue to Szerencs.

Szerencs

A strictly religious, Orthodox congregation was formed in the early nineteenth century in the one-time county seat. In 1929, the town had some 1400 Jewish inhabitants, ninety per cent of whom perished in the concentration camps and in the forced labour battalions.

The synagogue in Széchenyi Street was demolished; only the prayer-house (no longer in use) has survived at 50 Széchenyi Street. A memorial plaque and the walled cemetery preserves the memory of the flourishing Jewish community.

We continue our journey on Road 37.

Miskolc

The history of the Jewish community can be traced to the late eighteenth century. The first Jews lived on the nobles' estates – for example, we know about Jews who in 1717 opened a brandy (pálinka) tavern in Pál Szepessy's house, which was subsequently closed down by the town council. Later arrivals settled in Miskolc as the arendar of the inn and shop of the Diósgyőr estate. A cemetery was established by 1759 and a prayer-house by 1765, The community chose a rabbi and established a congregation. The Jews of Miskolc were primarily engaged in trade – they supplanted the Greeks, who had immigrated from Macedonia in the seventeenth century.

The oldest Jewish institution was the Chevra Kadisha, which on the testimony of the surviving documents, was formed in 1767. They founded a hospital in 1802. The Jews played a prominent role in the town's industrialisation, founding a number of factories and workshops. The first commercial school was founded by a Jewish teacher called Móric Strausz in 1848. Following Emperor Joseph II's edict, a Jewish "national" school was opened in 1784. This school was highly praised by Ferenc Kölcsey, one of the major poets and orators of the Enlightenment and author of the Hungarian national anthem, when he visited it in his capacity as a school-inspector. The so-called Erzsébet elementary school was built in 1900. The girls' gymnasium, founded in 1919, was relocated to a new building in 1926. There was a boys' gymnasium, three yeshivas and three Talmud-Torah schools. A teacher training school was established in 1928. There were three congregations, each with its own synagogue: a Status Quo, an Orthodox and a Sephardic one.

The town had a Jewish population of about fifteen thousand before the war. The Orthodox Israelite Congregation of Miskolc still maintains its synagogue, office building and other institutions. This is one of the few rural towns, which still has a ritual bath, and thus observant tourists can use the town as a base for exploring the northern and eastern part of Hungary.

The Orthodox great synagogue at 7 Kazinczy Street was built in 1863, according to the plans of the Viennese architect Ludwig Förster (who also designed the Dohány Street synagogue in Budapest). The large building, erected in line with the street, can be seen from afar. The façade is pierced by narrow, arched double windows set into a recessed frame, above which runs a decorative cornice. The main façade, with its triple, arched entrance decorated with handsome iron fittings, faces the courtyard. This synagogue has one of the most beautiful interiors in Hungary. The *bimah* stands in the centre. Seven steps lead to the raised Ark in the ornate eastern wall. The U shaped gallery with its raised railing is supported by slender, cast iron pillars. The hall has a roofing of large, painted, spandrel vaults.

The offices of the community, the butchery, the winter prayer room, the restaurant and other community premises can be found in the building constructed in the Eclectic style in the courtyard surrounding the synagogue. The plaque commemorating the victims of the Holocaust is set beside the entrance leading to the street behind the synagogue. The memorial plaque of the one-time teacher training college is located in the courtyard. An obelisk dedicated to the Jewish soldiers of the Great War, inscribed with a poem by Arnold Kiss (the one-time Chief Rabbi of Buda), stands in the centre of the courtyard. Visitors can find accommodation in the guesthouse near the synagogue.

The *mikveh* (ritual bath) near the Király Bridge was built in 1896.

The old cemetery lies is a beautiful setting, on the slope of Mt. Avas, at the end of Mendikás Road. The cemetery contains many old, nineteenth century graves, as well as the memorial to the victims of the Holocaust from Létrástető, Gadótanya, Ózd and Mezőkövesd.

Key to the maps

- synagogue
- prayer-house, prayer room
- Jewish community
- offices
- other Jewish buildings
- old age home, hospital
- school, kindregarten, Talmud-Torah
- culture hall, culture centre
- mikveh
- restaurant, buffet, cake shop
- hotel
- foodstore, butcher
- gift shop
- cemetery
- memorial
- place of pilgrimage
- communal kitchen, club
- office
- Orthodox
- Neolog
- kosher
- ruin
- non-Jewish use
- important monument
- listed monument
- not in use

Jewish sights and monuments in Budapest not mentioned in the text

Former Jewish community institutions

54. Girls' orphanage
(1071, 26 Damjanich Street)
55. Jewish Apprentice Home
(1071, 48 Damjanich Street)
56. Boys' orphanage
(1071, 25 Városligeti fasor)
57. Boys' orphanage
(1063, 10 Munkácsy Mihály Street)
58. Jewish Institute for the Deaf and Dumb
(1078, 2 Bethlen Gábor Square)
76. Jewish hospital
(1135, 33 Szabolcs Street)
78. Jewish gymnasium
(1146, 10 Cházár András Street)
79. Matzoh bakery
(1134, 26 Tüzér Street)
80. Hospital and nursing home of the Pest Chevra Kadisha (1145, 57 Amerikai Road)
81. Girl' orphanage
(1146, 149 Hungária Boulevard)
82. Old age home
(1146, 167 Hungária Boulevard)
110. Hospital of the Buda Chevra Kadisha
(1122, 16 Maros Street)
111. Bíró Dániel Hospital of the Budapest Orthodox Congregation (1122, 64–66 Városmajor Street)

Former synagogues

59. Orthodox prayer-house
(1076, 48 Garay Street)
86. Kőbánya synagogue
(1105, 7–9 Cserkesz Street)
113. Lágymányos synagogue
(1113, 37 Bocskay Road)
77. Angyalföld synagogue
(1134, 55 Dózsa György Road)
87. Rákospalota synagogue
(1047, 77 Fóti Road)
89. Rákoshegyi synagogue
(1174, 6 Podmaniczky Zsuzsanna Street)
88. Pestlőrinc synagogue
(1181, 8 Batthyány Lajos Street)
117. Nagytétény synagogue
(1225, 283 Nagytétényi Road)

Cemeteries in outlying districts

90. 1152, 111 Szentmihályi Road
91. 1162, 27 Bártfa Street
92. 1162, Rozsos Street
93. 1153, Pesti határ Road
94. 1164, Szabadföldi Road
95. 1173, Napkelet köz
96. 1172, Bártfai Street
97. 1175, Göcseji Road
98. Pestlőrinc
99. 1197, 6 Temető Street
100. 1237, Temető Row
101. 1195, 270 II. Rákóczi Ferenc Street
118. Nagytétény
119. 1118, 8 Temető Street (in the Catholic cemetery)

Memorials and memorial plaques

45. Ferenc Koszorús memorial plaque (1077, 1 Dohány Street)
46. Karl Lutz memorial (1074, corner of Dob and Rumbach Streets)
51. Ghetto memorial plaque (1077, 44 Wesselényi Street)
52. János Vázsonyi memorial plaque (1061, 2 Liszt Ferenc Square)
53. Plaque commemorating the murdered resistance fighters (1077, 52 Wesselényi Street)
60. Hanna Szenes Park and Memorial (1077, corner of Jósika and Rózsa Streets)
61. "Glass House" (1054, 29 Vadász Street)
62. Béla Stollár memorial plaque (1055, 2 Stollár Béla Street)
64. Friedrich Born memorial plaque (1051, 31 Arany János Street)
67. Plaque commemorating the Christian nuns and Jewish children shot into the Danube (1093, embankment by Közraktár Street)
68. Miklós Radnóti memorial plaque (1132, 6 Kádár Street)
69. Raoul Wallenberg Street and memorial plaque (1136, at the corner of Wallenberg and Pozsonyi Street)
70. Jewish resistance centre (1132, 36 Visegrádi Street)
71. Jewish resistance fighter's memorial plaque (1137, 35 Szent István Park)
72. Holocaust memorial (1137, Jászai Mari Square)

73. Giorgio Perlasca memorial plaque
(1137, Szent István Park)
74. Holocaust memorial plaque
(1133, 30 Vág Street)
75. Vizafogó memorial plaque and Mauthausen memorial (1133, Újpesti embankment)
83. Újpest memorial relief
(1042, 8 Berzeviczy Street)
84. Pesterzsébet memorial (1191, Templom Square)
85. Holocaust memorial in the cemetery
(1108, 6 Kozma Street)
103. Angelo Rotta memorial plaque
(1014, 6 Úri Street)
104. Gábor Sztehlo memorial plaque
(1014, Bécsi kapu Square)
105. Site of the Gestapo prison
(1027, 25 Gyorskocsi Street)
107. Imre Reviczky memorial plaque
(1024, Széna Square)
108. Plaque commemorating the one-time prison on Margit Boulevard (1024, Széna Square)
109. Raoul Wallenberg memorial
(1026, Szilágyi Erzsébet fasor)
112. Anti-Fascist memorial (1123, Gesztenyés Garden, beside the Budapest Congress Centre)
115. Memorial stone marking the site of the Óbuda Brick Factory (1032, 134 Bécsi Road)

Other Jewish relics

5. Jewish gravestones from the Roman Age in the Hungarian National Museum (1088, 14–16 Múzeum Boulevard)
63. Hebraica Collection of the Oriental Library of the Hungarian Academy of Sciences (1051, 7 Roosevelt Square)
116. Jewish gravestones from the Roman Age in the Aquincum Museum (1031, 139 Szentendrei Road)
106. Twelfth century Jewish gravestone in the Budapest History Museum (1014, 2 Szent György Square)

Contents

Preface 5
History of Hungarian Jewry 9
Gazetteer of Jewish institutions in Hungary 43
National Jewish organisations 44
Synagogues and synagogue districts in Budapest 45
Jewish communities and synagogues in the province 49
Central organisations 55
Societies, groups, associations 56
Schools, education 58
Culture 61
Journals and periodicals 62
Social institutions, old-age homes 64
Restaurants, gift shops, food stores 65
Burial 71
Suggested walks and sightseeing tours 73
Jewish sights and monuments in Budapest 73
The "synagogue triangle" (the former ghetto) 73
Other Jewish sights and monuments in Pest 89
Jewish sights and monuments in Buda 98
Óbuda 103
Jewish sights and monuments in the provinces 107
Western Hungary 108
The Balaton region 115
Southern Hungary 118
Along the Danube 123
The Great Hungarian Plain 128
Northern and eastern Hungary 140
The Pilgrim Route 142
Key to the maps 170
Jewish sights and monuments in Budapest
not mentioned in the text 171

The Bálint Jewish Community Center, located in the heart of Budapest, has been serving local Jewry since 1994.

This special place calls and awaits community members to understand, express and enjoy their Jewish culture, their Jewish tradition.

Bálint JCC gets in touch with more than 7000 families every month. The basic idea of its programming is to serve as a meeting point for different generations, for people with different interests and tastes.

It offers space for civil initiatives to grow, to meet each other and to connect with each other. It offers leisure time activities, cultural programs and sport activities. It brings the world to its members.

In Bálint JCC Jewish tradition can be practiced, learned and taught in a secular environment that is inviting for those who are unfamiliar with the world of the synagogues. The Center has an important role in observing the Jewish holidays. It cares for the Holocaust survivors and one of its main roles is to make the different generation meet and cooperate.

We would like to see you among our guests; please, get acquainted with our programs and be our guest!

Bálint Zsidó Közösségi Ház
1065 Budapest, Révay utca 16.
Telephone: 311-6669, 311-6667, 311-9218
www.jcc.hu

There is a place in Hungary where Jewish kids of 23 countries gather each year to spend 12 Jewish days together.

Szarvas

This place is waiting for your kid as well;
with well-trained, cheerful youth leaders,
with a tasteful Kosher kitchen, with pleasant lodging,
with a crystal-clear swimming pool, with tennis courts,
with air conditioned public spaces.

Lauder - JOINT

This place is capturing, this place is unforgettable – it is Szarvas, a starting point of new stories, new friendships and new fun.

Szarvas opens its gates every summer. Send your kids there – and call their friends, as well!

INTERNATIONAL JEWISH YOUTH CAMP

Find information on www.camp.jdc.hu,
or in JDC Office for Hungary
1075 Budapest, Síp utca 12.

CEU Graduate School of Business

Central European University, Budapest

The leading American Business School in Central-Eastern Europe, founded in 1988 by George Soros.

- Portfolio of New York licensed Management Degree Programs (MBA, Exec MBA, MSc IT)
- Joint Programs with top Western European Institutions
- International environment (multi-cultural student body from over 20 countries and global faculty)
- Strong links with corporate partners in Eastern Europe and Central Asia

www.gsb.ceu.hu

• CEU Graduate School of Business •

• H-1051 Budapest, Nádor u. 21, Hungary •

• Tel: + 36 1 327-3131 •

Jewish Studies AT CENTRAL EUROPEAN UNIVERSITY

BUDAPEST • HUNGARY

A specialization in Jewish Studies is offered as part of the Master's and doctoral degree programs of the Department of History and the Nationalism Studies Program. With a focus on the history and culture of Central and Eastern European Jewry, the Jewish Studies specialization offers a unique opportunity to study with renowned scholars in the heart of Central Europe. The specialization has been made possible by the generous support of the Yad Hanadiv Foundation and CEU.

For further information visit ***http://www.ceu.hu/jewish_studies.html*** or
contact the Program Coordinator, Szabolcs Pogonyi ***(pogonyi@ceu.hu)***.
The Jewish Studies Program is directed by Professor Andras Kovacs.

Central European University (CEU) is an internationally recognized, US degree granting institution of graduate education in the social sciences and humanities. CEU has an absolute charter from the Board of Regents of the University of the State of New York (US) for and on behalf of the New York State Education Department; the official language of instruction is English.

www.ceu.hu

Non-Discrimination Policy: Central European University does not discriminate on the basis of—including, but not limited to—race, color, national and ethnic origin, religion, gender or sexual orientation in administering its policies, admissions policies, scholarship and loan programs, and athletic and other school-administered programs.

Madách Dental
Dental Center

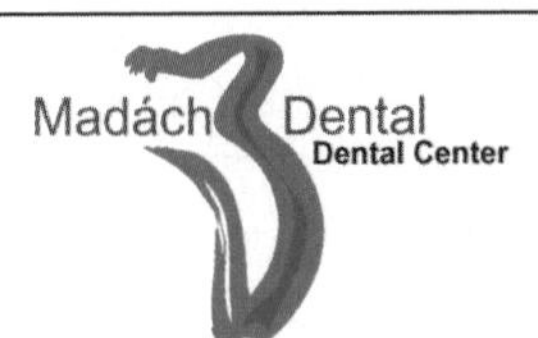

Full scope of dental services, e.g.:
- -dental prothesis, denture
- -implant of artificial roots
- -aesthetical dentistry
- -dental jewelry, whitening
- -dental plates, anaesthesia

16 dentists, 7 consulting rooms
friendly environment
in the heart of the city

FOR A BEAUTIFUL SMILE!

Consulting hours: each day 8 a.m. to 10 p.m.

Madách tér 7, Budapest 1075,mezzanine, phone:267-1600
www.madachdental.hu, e-mail: info@madachdental.hu

KLEZMER MUSIC LTD

H-1025 BUDAPEST, BATTAI U. 20/B.
FAX: (36-1) 275-1988

E-MAIL: AGI.BINDER@BUDAPESTKLEZMER.HU

HTTP//WWW.BUDAPESTKLEZMER.HU

CONCERTS, EVENTS

BE OUR GUEST!

International specialities • mainly Jewish foods
elegant atmosphere • first-class service
await you in

CARMEL CELLAR

Budapest, Kazinczy street 31.

OPENING HOURS:	*RESERVATIONS:*
Every day: 12–23 p.m.	3-221-834 • 3-424-585

The Restaurant has Air-Conditioning

Ophthalmology • Optometry
Tradition - Innovation • Eye-glasses
Sunglasses • Fashion Glasses
Contact Lenses

Specialized Shop • TÓBIÁS OPTIKA
Bem rakpart 53. Budapest 1027
(at the Buda abutment of Margit Bridge)
Phone/Fax: (36 1) 315-6115

Saloon • OPTIKA SINCE 1949
Rózsakert Shopping Mall
(102. 2nd floor)
Gábor Áron u. 74-78/a. I. em.,
Budapest 1026
Phone: (36 1) 391-5866
Phone/Fax: (36 1) 391-5867

Special Discounts,
wide range of spectacles

FRŐHLICH
CUKRÁSZDA

Open:
Monday–Thursday:
9 a.m.–6 p.m.
Friday:
7.30 a.m.– 4 p.m.
Sunday:
10 a.m.– 4 p.m.
Phone:
+ 36 1 267 2851

FRÖHLICH COFFEE-SHOP

The single kosher coffee-shop
in Hungary
Pastries of the
Austro-Hungarian Monarchy,
traditional Yiddish cakes,
exotic coffees

22 Dob Street (District VII)

MADAME GYÖRGYI'S

dating and matchmaking service

Our strength is our reliablity!

CALL NOW!

+36 1 326 5989

8 a.m.–10 a.m and
8 p.m.–10 p.m.

JEWELLERY
MADE FOR YOU

Gold, silver,
precious stones,
pearls
Individual designs
Judaica jewellery

MRS ZSUZSANNA HAVAS

CALL NOW!

+36 1 331 7831 or
+ 36 20 524 2881

Your reliable physician in Budapest

MEDICINA Betegség Megelőző Kft.

Tel.: +36 1 450 1889 • e-mail: miorvosunk@medicinabm.hu

Illness prevention and treatment:

- outpatient care
- full range of internal medicine and cardiology services
- medical tests necessary for residence and work permits
- employment health hazard evaluation services
- professional health-screening services for health insurance

Our highly qualified, English and German speaking staff provides professional care in a modern, well-equipped clinic

Biblical World Gallery and Shop
(next to Café Noé Jewish style coffee house)

The single **Jewish arts gallery**
in Eastern Europe offers Judaica, *antiques*,
gift items, jewelry from Israel,
as well as new and second-hand Jewish
books, music cassettes and CD's

Address:
H-1075 Budapest VII. Wesselényi u. 13.

Phone:
(36-1) 267-8502 Fax: (36-1) 354-1561
(Next to the diabetic cake shop, *Café Noé*)

Homepage and Internet shop:
www.zsido.hu and www.torta.hu

E-mail: makkabi@makkabi.hu